HIMALAYA VENTURE

FRITZ KOLB

Translated by Lawrence Wilson

Published by Sigma Leisure – an imprint of
Sigma Press, 1 South Oak Lane, Wilmslow, Cheshire SK9 6AR, England.

British Library Cataloguing in Publication Data
A CIP record for this book is available from the British Library.

ISBN: 1-85058-784-1

Typesetting and design: Sigma Press, Wilmslow, Cheshire.

Cover Design: The Agency, Macclesfield; based on the original cover illustration for 'Himalaya Venture'

Foreword

by Robey Johnson, one of the English members of the first Himalayan expedition described in this book

It was with great pleasure that I accepted the invitation to write a Foreword to this book, because it gives me the opportunity to introduce the author and his main companion in the expeditions described.

I first met them in Austria, when I was one of a group of beginners they were teaching to ski as part of the National Union of Students scheme for student holidays. How well I remember their patience and kindness; how obvious was the deep love of mountains and the adventurous spirit which later led to their Himalayan trips.

What a complementary pair they were. Fritz, with his seemingly inexhaustible supply of patience and good humour, encouraging the weary with cheerful word and helping hand. Ludwig with his boundless energy, estimating the difficulties and making decisions backed by experience and careful thought. Was it any wonder that I caught some of the infectious enthusiasm of such friends?

Looking back, I can see how the first trip must have cramped their natural style. How they must have chafed at our insensibility to the need to "scorn delights and live laborious days". How well they concealed their urge to go twice as far, in half the time, on half a shoestring.

They must have had to make a difficult decision after the dramatic arrival of the news of the outbreak of war. There they were, sitting near a mountain-top more than half-way to Tibet, with their friends the enemy. Should they turn south for India and a concentration camp, or northward towards Tibet and the great unknown? It is interesting to speculate what greater epic journeys they might have made if they had chosen the second alternative. As it was they went off to long weary years of internment, to dream of their beloved mountains and to keep alive the determination to go back. The book shows how well they succeeded.

What they managed to do with so little time and money, underlines the tremendous opportunities for small parties travelling light in the Himalayas, and may encourage other adventurous spirits to do likewise.

Robey Johnson, 1957

Contents

CHAPTER 1

The Friendly Enemies

IN the 1930s, experience of mountain climbing was not enough to include a citizen of the Third Reich in one of the big Himalayan Expeditions; other, less relevant qualifications were required. And, even if he possessed them, the applicant still had to pull strings to get selected from the large numbers applying. Failing that, the only possibility was a private expedition, but most people could not afford the expenditure involved unless they obtained an assignment from a newspaper or a film company. Many enterprising enthusiasts managed to get sponsored in this way. Others found the necessary time and money by becoming professional globe-trotters and writing travel books. Those who had no influential friends in the right places, no talent for raising funds and no desire to sacrifice their existing career stayed at home – of those staying at home, I was one.

But though I had thrust from me the thought of reaching the Himalayas, I could not stop dreaming about them. I avoided all mountaineering books, reports of expeditions, travellers' tales, but, whenever I saw a large-scale map of mountains like Nanga Parbat with blanks where the territory was unexplored, the old fever returned.

Such maps were a speciality of my friend, Ludwig Krenek. As he appears throughout this story, Ludwig deserves a formal introduction. Dear boy, he was a bit on the short side, but he could jump like a kangaroo and his leg muscles never tired. He loved the sun and the sun loved him – his bronzed skin never got burnt. His features suggested energy, good humour and no more than a laudable trace of ambition. He seemed to know every star in the sky, from galaxy to spiral nebula, from the Little Bear to the Southern Cross, while background, foreground, focus, aperture and shutter speed and all else to do with the finer points of photography were second nature to him. Temperamentally, Ludwig was an Oriental – he possessed the enviable ability to concentrate on the job in hand to the entire exclusion of his surroundings. Any headmaster who had Ludwig Krenek among his schoolteachers could count himself lucky. His pupils would do anything for him and some whom I met twenty years after they had left school were still full of his praises.

Ludwig and I were old friends. We had done some tough climbing together and in the 1930s we found ourselves teaching at the same secondary school in Vienna. As a matter of course in the summertime, we conspired to hold our classes out of doors on the slopes of the Vienna woods. In the summer holidays and at Christmas and Easter we used to act as guides to parties of British students visiting the Austrian Alps. After the first World War the National Union of Students had set up an office in Vienna[1] and here, steadily and quietly, a great contribution was made to international understanding. Thousands of British students, teachers and medical men were put in touch with their colleagues in Austria and, in particular, the Union sponsored expeditions on which British students went climbing under the supervision of experienced Austrian students or teachers in every part of Austria and, later, in Switzerland and the Near East. It was from the N.U.S. centre that Ludwig used to bring those disturbing maps.

As one of these student ventures, Ludwig and I had often toyed with the idea of organising a trip to Afghanistan. It seemed at first sight quite feasible; other guides had already taken parties as far as Persia. But, going by motor-coach, they had had a large number of participants to share the travelling expenses of the guides who went free of charge. On the other hand, a climbing expedition – which was the only kind of expedition that interested us – would not only be more expensive than a coach trip, but would have to be limited to a maximum of four students – two novices to each experienced mountaineer – and, as our young Englishmen seldom came from wealthy families, we could not expect to get a party of the usual type together.

So for a while we shelved the idea, until one morning in the winter of 1937, during a break between classes, I suggested to Ludwig another scheme. I told him we should try and find four

---

[1] Die Akademisch-soziale Arbeitsgemeinschaft.

young Englishmen who would be prepared to live as simply and cheaply in the Himalayas as we did on our own trips in the Austrian Alps. No hotels, not even rest-houses, but tents – three Sherpas instead of the usual twelve – twenty or thirty villagers instead of two hundred as porters to the base camp – no oxygen apparatus or other special Himalayan equipment. Tents and sleeping-bags could be borrowed from the Union. As we could not expect to obtain special leave from school, the trip would have to last no more than twelve weeks and be fitted into the summer holidays. We should have to travel as cheaply as possible, which probably meant a return ticket to Bombay in an Italian boat. Finally, Ludwig and I should have to save all we could for a year or even two years so that as far as possible we could cover the expenses of the expedition ourselves.

Of course, cutting down on time and equipment would rule out any 25,000-foot mountains as our objective. We should have to content ourselves with 20,000-footers, and of those there should be some within quick reach of Bombay. I reckoned that the sea trip alone would take up a whole fortnight each way.

Ludwig listened glumly. "We should have to get there before the monsoon and that is long before our holidays," was all he said, but that did not worry me. I knew Ludwig and was sure he would continue to revolve the idea in his mind. So we went back to our classrooms and while he put ticks, crosses and an occasional irate NO! against untidy sums, I explained, drawing on unlimited reserves of patience, when German orthography required a small "s", when a capital and when a peculiar form written thus: ß.

Four times a week Ludwig and I came up for air in geography classes, a subject which we both taught. One day we continued it privately in the break. Ludwig had got hold of some maps of the Himalayas, or rather of a part north of Simla in Lahul which seemed to offer just what we wanted. The area was partially unexplored and it was protected from the monsoon by a more southerly chain of mountains. Its highest point was given on the map as 21,380 feet. This mountain lay roughly in the centre of the area. Its height had been calculated by trigonometry. It was unnamed on the map and no attempt had ever been made to climb it. To reach it from Bombay would take a week, which was well within the time limit imposed by the school holidays. Nothing could be better! Now for the practical side.

First, we worked out the cost of the trip and then we tried to find four young Britons who could afford it. That was not easy, but at last we had our team. "If I can stay alive for two years on bread and cheese, I might just about make it," wrote Johnny, whom we had met skiing in the Tyrol. Robey Johnson was his name and he taught at a London secondary school.

Our next recruit was Frank Hollick, a friend of Ludwig's from Cambridge, and the third, Miss Hilda Richmond, also a school-teacher, from Leeds. Our fourth was to have been a seasoned Alpine mountaineer, but at the last moment he was unable to come. His place was taken by Donald Comber, a student from Windsor who had only just passed his twentieth birthday. His father had agreed to pay his expenses.

With the team complete, Ludwig and I started to save so that we could pay our share of the cost. That was in 1937. By August 1939 we had saved enough and the main party of our expedition was ready to embark at Venice for India. August 1939: for most people they were the last days of peace, but for us they were the first of our Himalayan adventure.

*   *   *   *

Ludwig was organizer-in-chief and he decreed that, with Frank Hollick, whom I had not yet met, I was to go on a fortnight ahead of the others to prepare the way. This was necessary in order to save time, for even those of us with three months' holiday would only have a bare four weeks in the mountains, the rest of the time being taken up with travel.

So, after a final consultation with Ludwig, I left Vienna by train for Marseilles on the evening of July 12. My wife came to see me off and, as the train moved out, I stood waving to her from a corridor window. Then the coaches swung round a curve and the last tip of her handkerchief vanished. Soon the suburbs were flitting past and the other third-class passengers began to settle themselves for the night. I stayed at the window. I could hear their chatter, but was not yet ready to join it. Was war really coming? Would it come while I was away from home? I planned to return on November 1; until then my wife had arranged to stay in England. We had done many hard climbs together and she would have been with me now if we could have afforded the double passage to India.

The money I had with me amounted to 150 French francs and

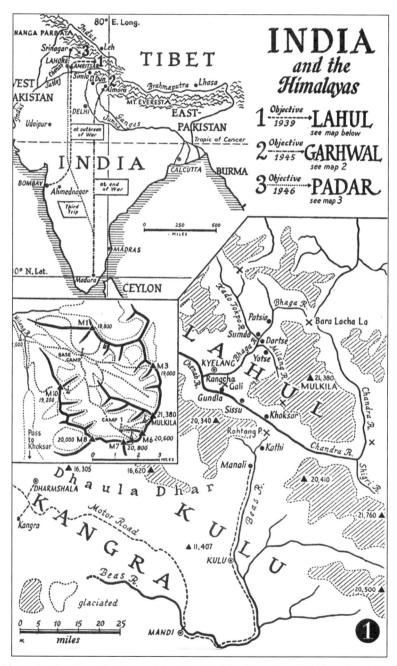

Maps showing the author's expeditions into the Himalayas. Detailed Maps 2 and 3 can be found on pages 69 and 91 respectively

6 reichsmarks. When travelling abroad, even when travelling as far as the Himalayas, I had been told that a citizen of the Greater German Reich might take with him only 10 marks' worth of foreign exchange or 10 marks in German money, but not both. I was therefore due to surrender my 6 marks when we reached the Italian frontier at Arnoldstein. My return passage to India had been paid in advance by the Union of Students through the clearing agreement, and the sterling Ludwig and I would need in India would be provided by our British friends in payment for mountaineering equipment which we would supply. Meanwhile I thought I could manage on 150 French francs.

But I had reckoned without the fall of the Bastille. I arrived at Marseilles on July 14 and 149 francs and 70 centimes went in taxi fares and tips before I could get hold of an official to clear my luggage through the Customs. After that, I had to reach the docks where the splendiferous *Strathnaver* beckoned like some unattainable eldorado. My last 30 centimes would take me and my luggage to within sight of the docks, but no further, and I had to walk the rest of the way, dragging my heavy suitcases after me. Eventually, with many pauses for rest, I reached the ship where I was to make the acquaintance of my English companion, Frank Hollick.

Frank was a biologist and worked at Cambridge University. He was then twenty-seven and I, the oldest of the party, thirty-seven. He and Ludwig had done long trips together in the Ötztaler Alps and, as a result, Ludwig had invited him to come with us to the Himalayas. But, as our very first conversation showed, Frank was more scientist at heart than mountaineer. Within an hour, he had me embroiled on the fundamentals of the scientific method and all the topical -isms: empiricism, a-priori-ism, logical positivism. Thence, without a break, to quantum-physics, the irregularities in the behaviour of the electron and their effect, if any, on the validity of determinism. Frank had recently graduated and at that time, of course, at the dawn of the Atomic Age, was at the vortex of the scientific maelstrom. I, on the other hand, had studied philosophy with a Viennese friend who has since acquired an international reputation and had shared in the travail of producing his first published work. So Frank and I had interests in common, enough, at any rate, for us to agree on the requirements which a scientific proposition must fulfil if it is to have validity. And

what else mattered? Oh, yes! Complete intellectual honesty....
Also agreed! We beamed. What a splendidly supra-national
thing, this modern science!

But I had to admit that the aquatic creatures Frank hoped to
catch in the Himalayas for the British Museum were a closed
book to me, though he found me a responsive guinea-pig for
some theories he was working out on the flight of insects, a
subject to which he devoted himself, day in, day out, while our
gleaming white ship was thrusting powerfully across the blue
waters of the Mediterranean.

At Port Said, we entered a new and colourful world, and we
were not the first to be fascinated by the journey through the
Suez Canal. Among our fellow passengers was a young Indian
girl who had been to school in England and was now on her way
home with her mother. Small and dainty, with a sweet face
framed in smooth, raven-black hair, she wore the *sari* over a
white blouse with puffed sleeves – sometimes a length of
brilliant green silk spangled with stars, at others a pure white
sari with a brocaded border woven into the material. Frank and I
became friendly with this charming girl and each day she helped
us with our Hindustani.

roti – bread

pani – water

roti mangta – I would like some bread

ao – come!

jáo – go!

Kal – yesterday

"And 'tomorrow'?" I asked.

"The same word – *kal*," was the surprising reply.

We passed through the Red Sea and after calling at Aden met
heavy weather in the Indian Ocean. The south-west monsoon
was blowing at full strength, the warm, moisture-laden winds
driving night and day towards the parched land-masses of India.
In the high mountains in the north, it would be snowing. Would
the lower ranges really take all the moisture from the clouds, I
wondered? Would we find tolerable weather beyond, in the
mountains of Lahul?

As the ship heaved and rolled in the steep seas, the dining
saloon began to empty, more and more of the passengers lying
cocooned in misery in deck-chairs on the upper deck. The

captain did what he could. He had a glass screen erected to shield them from the wind and spray, and the ship's band were given orders to play gay tunes wherever they saw green faces. But Bombay and dry land were the only permanent cure.

*   *   *   *

An unpleasant surprise awaited us in Bombay. The certificate we had obtained from the India Office in London exempting our equipment from Customs duty was not accepted as no "confirmation" had been received from Delhi. Argument proved useless; we had to pay the full duty and content ourselves with an official assurance that the money would be refunded when we left India. Meanwhile, if our main party suffered the same fate, we should all be bankrupt before we reached the Himalayas.

Frank and I decided that he should go to Simla, the summer seat of government, to try and ensure that our friends' luggage was allowed through the Customs duty-free, under the normal tourist concessions, while I went on to Amritsar to arrange for the expedition's food supplies. Together we set off by train, across the limitless plains of India and all I recall is that Frank stepped off somewhere during a journey that lasted two nights and a day.

Until a few days before I left Vienna we had been uncertain whether the trip would come off, hence we had been late and somewhat half-hearted in making detailed preparations. At the last moment we had tried to find out where in India we could buy food supplies for the expedition, but had started the journey before we received replies to our letters. Of course, we could have bought all we needed in Bombay, but the freight charges northwards would have been beyond our means and it was therefore essential to buy food as close as possible to the scene of operations. It seemed doubtful whether the smaller places in the mountains, such as Kangra, Dharmshala and Kulu, could supply us, but I intended to have a good look round in Amritsar, the nearest sizeable town.

The train reached Amritsar at 6 a.m. and I emerged more dead than alive from an overcrowded compartment where I had spent most of the night talking to a Mohammedan professor of political economy from Delhi. As the shops were not yet open, I decided to locate the Imperial Bank of India and some of the more likely stores, and then make up for lost sleep on a park bench.

In the town, I found rows of one-storey houses and plenty of shops. As well as my stupor would allow, I studied the signs. Most of them were in the Devangari script or in Urdu with an English translation beneath. Soon the day's business began and where the signs were uninformative, I judged the type of shop from the goods displayed. Flour, corn, peas, lentils, sugar and salt were plentiful and I could also have bought a Singer sewing machine or a bicycle – in fact, almost anything but the food without which it was thought in those days no one could survive in the Himalayas: condensed milk, tinned jam, corned beef, bacon, biscuits, dried fruit, crispbread, soup tablets and the rest.

I could see a small park at the far end of the town, so I followed the drift of the crowd towards it, jostling my way slowly along side-alleys without finding the kind of shop I was looking for. At last, I found myself gazing at a lake and a wonderful building reflected in it – the Golden Temple, the sacred shrine of the Sikhs. For a while I stood by the lake; then I continued the search for a European grocer among thickening throngs of haggling shoppers, weaving my way past endless bazaars, skirting shadowy doorways where figures squatted, impassively smoking the hookah, all the while taking in a profusion of strange wares – fruit I had never seen before, leather goods, wooden implements, cloth, brass bowls engraved with complicated patterns – till once more I emerged from the town on a different side and saw dusty trees, taxis and motor lorries.

Feeling peevish and discouraged, I collapsed on the nearest bench. Graceful tree-rats with bushy tails came hopping up to inspect me. My feet ached, my eyes smarted and my stomach twinged.

Towards ten o'clock I called a cab and told the driver to take me to a barber. "*Hajam ko chaláo!*" Whether it was the words or my gesture, rubbing a hand over my bearded chin, that he understood hardly mattered – he took me to a barber, the cab bumping along beside the town wall, through the gateway and into the street I had first entered that morning. The barber's shop was one of the first we came to. With the beard, I lost some of my ill humour. In halting English the barber explained where the bank was and assured me there were no shops in Amritsar that sold tinned food.

First, I went to the Imperial Bank of India. The main hall was a hive of activity, the air fairly humming with murmured conversations between customers and clerks. With my naïve conceptions of "British" India, I was surprised to see none but Indian faces behind the grilles. A Sikh counted me out 300 silver coins, ringing each one on the marble slab. At that time, no one in India would have dreamt of accepting a single rupee before making sure it was genuine and later on we, too, kept to the rule, though more so as not to lose face than because any of us would have spotted the difference in tone if we had rung a counterfeit coin.

Inside the bank, soldiers with sloped arms were patrolling to and fro, but I noticed they stopped and stared at me when they heard the ting-a-ling of 300 rupees. With nameless fears springing from my ignorance of the country, I quickly dropped the bagful of silver into my briefcase and left the building. In the street outside I bought a bunch of bananas and stilled the worst of my hunger. Then I plucked up courage and went into one of the wretched food-shops. The owner spoke not a word of English. At the next shop I was luckier. I could make myself understood and the man actually stocked tinned food. There was little variety, but he was an enterprising man and promised to obtain every item I asked for in quantities to last the six of us for a month.

I was soon in a position to tell the main party what they should buy in Bombay and what could be obtained in Amritsar, and after enquiries in Kulu, further to the north, I wrote to Ludwig telling him, amongst other details, that prices in Bombay, Amritsar and Kulu were in the proportion 100–127–156.

From Amritsar, the train took me another two hours' journey to the northern edge of the Indian plain. Then at Pathankot the first hills appeared. Two motor buses, or rather, lorries, were on the point of starting for Kangra. I wedged myself in among a colourful throng of men, women and children and we set off. Soon we reached an up-gradient and the road started winding in steep curves and sharp corners. Looking back, we had a splendid view of the Kangra River where it left a rocky gorge and stepped sedately out into the plain. All was bathed in warm evening sunshine. The passengers began to sing. Still we climbed between wooded slopes and walls of rock, the driver skilfully negotiating the bends and keeping most conscientiously, I thought, to his side of the road. Later I saw why: at each bend the centre line was planted with small boulders.

Soon after sunset it was completely dark. We drove on through a number of villages where fires glowed through the open doorways of the huts. Sometimes the lorry behind us went ahead for a while, then dropped back again. As we were crossing open fields, our driver suddenly pulled up with a jerk – a party of apes on the road.

We reached Kangra at about 9 p.m. I jumped down and enjoyed the relief of stretching my legs. Then I called out: "Does anyone here understand English?" A young man said he did.

"Is there a hotel in this place?"

"No."

"A *dak* bungalow?"

"Yes."

"Where?"

"A mile from here."

"Could you help me find a porter to carry my luggage there?"

The young man said certainly, and within a matter of seconds my suitcase was perched on the head of a porter and we were off into the night. At first my guide led me between huts, then came a road that ran diagonally across a slope covered with brush-wood. Finally, a steep path led us up to the hill-top where the rest-house was sited.

After some time the *chawkidar* (caretaker) appeared and after a further wait I had my tea with bread and butter. The porter had long since gone home. Soon I was saying good night and shutting my door. I lay down on the *chárpái* (bed), turned over once, then slept long and soundly far on into a morning of brilliant sunshine.

While waiting for breakfast, I inspected my beautiful surroundings. The rest-house stood on a spur with steep, wooded slopes and the river curling gracefully at their foot. Beyond, in the plain, lay fields of maize and rice, tea plantations and an occasional cluster of houses approached by a road flanked with trees. To northward, the plain was bounded by an imposing wall of mountains, their peaks hidden by thick cloud – the Dhaula Dhar Range.

When I returned in the autumn the peaks were visible, but though the Dhaula Dhar Mountains rise 12,000 feet above the plain their effect on me was no greater than those behind Innsbruck, which are only half as high above the town. But the Dhaula Dhar peaks are rather tame in outline and the snow covering is too sparse to throw the grey-green of the escarpment into relief. Of course, the peaks were a magnificent sight, but seen from Kangra, the southern aspect of the Himalayas did not quite come up to my expectations. To see them to best advantage one has to go to Darjeeling, Mussoorie or Almora.

All the *dak* bungalows which I saw in this part of India had been sited in spots carefully selected for their picturesque surroundings. They are spaced at intervals of a day's journey, are run by the government and have a uniform tariff. The furnishing of the rooms is also standard and consists of a table with chairs, two or three beds made of webbing stretched between wooden frames, a paraffin lamp, an earthenware jug for drinking water, one or two books for light reading and a *gusl khana* – that is, a small wash-room.

After serving a plentiful breakfast, the *chawkidar* presented me with a piece of cardboard on which a police notice was pinned. The notice was dated August 1939 and called on all persons not of British nationality to report to the nearest police station within twenty-four hours.

Feeling rested and energetic, I went back to Kangra. It was a Tuesday. Frank was due to arrive from Simla on the following day. Meanwhile, there was a lot to do. In particular, I wanted to inform the police of our plans so that we would not be held up when entering the state of Lahul. Outside the police station in Kangra some brown fellows armed with rifles, tough-looking customers, gaped at me as I passed between them to the door. Inside, there were more of them crouching on the floor. At the table, with a wooden truncheon in front of him, sat the captain of police. Not a white face anywhere! When he saw me the captain jumped to his feet and roared out a command, whereupon every-one stood up stiffly to attention with eyes front. Trying not to look surprised, I pulled myself together and gestured vaguely. Then the good people all sat down again.

It turned out that the only person who could speak English was a melancholy scribe who was seated cross-legged in a corner of the room, busily tracing a long story in Urdu on sheets of paper spread round him on the floor. I gathered from him that the police in Kangra knew nothing about the notice I had been shown. Was he sure, I asked? The scribe consulted the captain, and the captain shook his head like a small boy accused of stealing apples. Surely, I thought, this man can't be chief of police for a whole district? No, as it turned out, he wasn't. The District Commissioner lived higher up, where it was cooler.

When I told the officer I would go next day to Dharmshala – it was only a few miles away and on the bus route from Kangra – he looked greatly relieved, for that saved him the trouble of thinking what to do about the strange Sahib who insisted on obeying a police notice which he, the police captain, had never heard of.

Dharmshala was more like a European town. After a fitting interval, I was allowed to enter the District Commissioner's office. He turned out to be a friendly Scot. He knew all about the notice and told me bluntly he already had a list of people in his District whom he would have to arrest on the outbreak of war. Fritz Kolb and Ludwig Krenek would be added. Then, as though to soften the blow, he told me he was very fond of football and thought highly of the Vienna First XI. And there, on the wall, was a photograph of the team he himself had once played in. By the way, had I ever been to Munich? So had he, on a business trip. Would I recognize this? The Commissioner went to a cupboard and pulled out a genuine Bavarian *Joppe*, the famous grey jacket with green facings. The flood-gates of reminiscence were now wide open, but the time for the last bus was also getting near and reluctantly I had to remind the Commissioner that I needed a pass so that our expedition could enter Lahul. He got up at once and in a moment returned with the document. I thanked him. "Not at all," he said, then added with a smile: "*Auf Wiedersehen!*"

The bus took me down the winding road into Kangra, where I found Frank with the glad news that his trip to Simla had been completely successful.

* * * *

On August 10, 1939, Frank Hollick, myself, a cook, a drover and three horses laden with baggage reached Kyelang, the principal village of Lahul. We had come up the much-frequented caravan route from Manali, where the road from Kangra ends, over the Rohtang Pass and through the Upper Chandra Valley, having an uneventful journey except that, at the south end of the pass, we awoke one morning to find our pack-horses had made off during the night. After some fuming and fretting, we had then come upon the obliging Mohammed with three unladen horses and Frank had persuaded him to transport our baggage to Lahul. While they were parleying, I had raced the gathering monsoon clouds to the top of the pass to take photographs, and I was horrified when I got there to find myself overcome with mountain sickness. Yet, the height was only 13,000 feet. How should I fare, I wondered, when we reached the real mountains? But the sickness must have been due to the speed of our climb and the rapid change in altitude, for it did not recur.

Kyelang lies north of the first great Himalayan ranges – those ranges in fact, which Ludwig was relying on to protect us from the worst of the monsoon. To meet the author of a favourite book, say, may or may not be a pleasant surprise, but it is always a surprise. So it was with Kyelang. For over two years, Ludwig and I had bandied about the name and we could draw from memory a map of the mountains, passes and rivers in the region. Inevitably, we formed a vaguely Asiatic picture of this place, so its appearance in real life was rather unexpected; when twilight veiled the castor oil bushes, the cypresses and the rest of the unfamiliar vegetation, I might have been in some broad Alpine valley. The village stood on a terrace high above the Bhaga River. On both sides of the valley, long green slopes led up to broken yellow stone. Upstream, great humps of ice peered above blue-grey mountain shoulders; downstream, some beautifully shaped, lightly glaciated peaks stood out against the sky. With the snow-line as high as it was in this region, their 16,000 to 17,000 feet should be no harder to climb, I thought, than some of the 12,000-foot peaks in the Alps.

For over 100 years, the Evangelical Church of the Moravian Brotherhood had maintained a mission in Kyelang for the propagation of the Christian Faith among the Lahulis. At the time of our visit, the mission was run by the Reverend F. A. Peter and his sister, Elizabeth Peter. They were the only white people in the whole of Lahul. Mr. Peter was a young man with an athletic figure and a smiling, energetic expression. The walls of his house were hung with trophies of the chase and the floors covered with the skins of wild animals. He was much in demand among the local people and had often to act as doctor and judge as well as priest.

Two bridges over the Bhaga River *(Ludwig Krenek)*

Mr. Peter had accompanied a well-known Asian explorer on his travels and he knew a good deal about climbing. He told us he had been given the job of supervising the baggage porters – not an easy one, for they were all convinced that the expedition was completely pointless. Why risk your life among the glaciers of the Karakorum, they argued, where there was no game to be shot and not even sheep could find grazing? And why risk provoking the gods of the Himalayan peaks by trespassing on their abode? Thus, the porters were never enthusiastic and when the danger became too great, or the route too arduous, or the distance from their homes exceeded a certain limit, they would lay down their 60-pound loads and tell the Sahib that they had no use for his money and were now returning to their villages. The Sahib would then be helpless indeed!

"Without the Asiatics' frugality and capacity for self-denial, none of the big Himalayan expeditions would have been possi-

Donald Comber, Fritz Kolb, Elizabeth Peter and her brother The Rev. F. A. Peter, Frank Hollick and Ludwig Krenek *(Ludwig Krenek)*

ble," said the missionary. "Their backs were free to carry the white men's baggage because all they needed for a fortnight's journey was one blanket and a small bag of roasted barley flour."

I had started the conversation by asking Mr. Peter whether the Lahuli, who was later to ply regularly between the mission house and our base camp, would need a tent to sleep in at night. The missionary had smiled and assured me that the man would flatly refuse to drag a tent around with him because he would never use it, preferring to sleep under a tree. Incidentally, the only regular link between Kyelang and the outside world was a Post Office runner who took letters twice a week over the Rohtang Pass. There was no telegraph, telephone or radio.

Frank and I kept thinking of more questions to put to the Reverend Peter and he patiently answered them all. He and his sister gave us every imaginable help, from taking regular

Left: Hilda Richmond and Robey Johnson; right: Shankr Singh and Ang Tsering
(Ludwig Krenek)

readings of the aneroid barometer for our subsequent altitude survey to buying food for us locally and sending it on with fruit and vegetables from their own garden. Thanks to the information he gave us, Frank and I felt a good deal more confident when, two days later, we continued our journey northward.

For the first day we followed the Simla-Leh caravan route; then we entered unexplored mountain territory, pushing on fifteen miles further north to a height of 10,900 feet and the junction of the rivers Bhaga, Kado Tokpo and Milang at the village of Sumdo. Lying at the mouth of the Milang Valley, which leads straight to the highest mountains in Lahul, Sumdo was the ideal base for further reconnaissance. We could not use the mule path, as it led up the Bhaga Valley to the Bara Lacha Pass and thence to Leh in the Upper Indus Valley, so we discharged Mohammed and his three pack-horses, deciding to rely in future on porters from the hamlets of Sumdo, Dartse and Yotse.

Our sole servant was now the cook, Shankr Singh. We had liked him from the start. He could convey almost anything with his fifteen words of English, and when we had learnt fifteen words of Hindustani we got on even better. Thanks to him, the inhabitants of Sumdo allowed us to set up our tents in a shady garden.

The laden mule caravan in the Chandra Valley *(Ludwig Krenek)*

It was now up to me to reconnoitre the 21,500-foot mountain that Ludwig and I had long ago noted from the map as the highest point in Lahul, and to find out if it had a name and also how we should approach it. Meanwhile, Frank intended to search for specimens of a certain rare breed of water-beetle. If he could find some and convey them intact to the British Museum in London, he had been guaranteed a small contribution towards his expenses. When we left Sumdo at the end of a week, he had, in fact, managed to make a complete collection of the insects to be found in the Kado Tokpo River, amounting to some hundreds of different species, and had a specimen of each neatly encased in a match-box with the appropriate label. In many cases, he was able to record a complete life-history of the creatures as well, with details of their birth, growth, reproductive and feeding habits entered in a separate note-book.

As I gazed at Frank's well-ordered cemetery, I suddenly realized why he had wanted to buy a pair of gumboots in Bombay, or rather, what "gumboots" were. At the time, my English vocabulary had not encompassed such exotic terms and from his description I had gathered he wanted a pair of sewerman's boots. It seemed odd, particularly as sewers are hard to find in India, but as Frank seemed normal in other respects, I felt I ought to give him the benefit of the doubt. I had congratulated myself at the time on restraining my impatience as Frank vainly sought gumboots in shop after shop. Now, as he stood barefoot for hours each day, up to his knees in icy glacier-water, I felt bitter remorse. Frank, if only I had helped you to find gumboots in Bombay!

Just behind Sumdo was a mountain of 15,093 feet, which the villagers called Bilhamo. From the summit I hoped to get a good view up the Milang Valley, but on my first attempt the weather got steadily worse as I climbed the mountain, and when I reached the summit I could see nothing. On the second attempt, the visibility was excellent and I stayed on the summit for a good six hours, drawing and busying myself with camera and theodolite. The only interruption was an aggressive eagle which gave me one bad fright. From Bilhamo the central range of the Himalayas lay spread before me, and near at hand, rearing above the Milang Valley, I could see "our" mountain – a beautiful, gleaming ice-peak, well named by the villagers Mulkila, which means Silver God. The god was surrounded by mighty courtiers all decked in shimmering ice. I hoped we should be able to reach the foot via the village of Yotse.

Mulkila, the highest mountain in Lahul, seemed well chosen as the goal of our expedition. Further to the north, despite their considerable height, the mountains were not so bold in outline and the ice-cover was less – an effect, no doubt, of the dry climate of Central Asia. To the south, in Kulu, the mountains were wild enough, but the monsoon broke against them with all its force. In central Lahul, on the other hand, the mountains were just hard enough to climb and for us, who could spare only a very few days in which to get acclimatized, they were at just the right height above sea-level. Finally, the weather was often fine and seldom really bad.

Until now, I had been secretly fearing that the mountains of Lahul would not prove wild and difficult enough to satisfy our mountaineering ambitions. That fear had now gone, to be replaced by a more insidious threat to my own private urge to scale ice and rock. From the summit of Bilhamo I could see, twisting along the mountain slopes below me, pathways that had been used for thousands of years by horses, mules, yaks, sheep

Clockwise from left: men, women and children from Lahul (*Ludwig Krenek*)

and goats. Following the beaten track to the pass at the head of the valley, men and animals were forced to rest there because of the altitude, and the first green patch they came to on the far side of the pass, with the first juniper bushes, had been the spot they had always chosen, for thousands of years, to set up their camp. Having rested, they would continue on down the valley, after some days reach a village, then come to another river, go toiling uphill to another pass, knowing that beyond Leh, when they reached it, the great Karakorum Range began, then the Pamirs and beyond them the vast, the measureless steppes of South Russia.

Life is hard in these parts of Asia, and so it was here in Lahul. In Sumdo the traveller sees the last trees, the last fields of barley, the last few blades of grass before he reaches the Bara Lacha Pass, and they only grow because the villagers have diverted a stream to water them. It hardly ever rains. Yet the people are cheerful; they love to sing and wear bright colours; they are artistic and they possess character. They treat their horses and dogs as friends and their minds are open to another, spiritual world of which we Europeans can sense little or nothing.

These things, and the hollow moaning of the afternoon wind, the rustle of the streams and the tinkling sheep-bells lay a spell on the traveller which sooner or later proves irresistible, and during that week in Sumdo I realized for the first time that there was a distinction to be drawn between those travellers like ourselves who came to the Himalayas athirst for mountaineering

glory and those others who cared nothing for climbing, but felt the lure of the country and spent the rest of their lives there, travelling and exploring. For myself I now knew that I belonged to neither type, or perhaps to both; I was somewhere in the gulf between the two. I have been there ever since.

*　　*　　*　　*

On the afternoon of August 19, Frank and I started repacking our baggage into manageable loads, intending to get closer to our mountain on the following day. While we were still at work Shankr came to tell us that "big lady" was on her way to Sumdo. For the last two days I had noticed preparations for some kind of festivity, but when I asked Shankr why the lady was coming, he replied: "To see you!" We were

greatly intrigued, particularly when we saw the visitor, a Lahuli woman of undeniable dignity and a certain raffish charm. So as not to interrupt our work, we took it in turns to converse with her, which we did by signs. We offered her some sweets, which she accepted, but then passed on with a condescending expression to her female attendant. The lady had her four-year-old son with her and he had, of course, to be included in the conversation. While the bystanders kept up a hum of comment, I showed mother and son my Zeiss binoculars. Then Frank demonstrated his microscope. We were both an enormous success, so successful that I was afraid we would never get away.

Frank Hollick's zoological specimens *(Frank Hollick)*

As it was beginning to get dark and we had still some packing to do, I felt it was time to part, amicably but firmly. The difficulty was to tear our visitors away from Frank's microscope. In order to get them moving, I invited the gracious lady to examine our tent. But the distinction between a brief glance and a prolonged stay proved beyond my power to convey in sign language and it was clear that my gestures were misunderstood. Drawing on the stock-in-trade of her sex, the lady gave one of those coyly reproving smiles that women everywhere reserve for the froward male and at the same time shook her head vigorously. "No! No!", interpreted a grinning bystander. "She will not sleep with you in the tent, but up there as a guest of the village!"

Early next morning – it was August 20, 1939 – we set off accompanied by seven native porters to move further up the Milang Valley and reconnoitre a suitable site for a base camp whence to attack the 20,000-foot peaks. The River Milang is fed by two streams and, when we reached the confluence, we found we were on the wrong bank to reach the triangle of land which lay between them and which led to the main glacier in the region. There was no bridge and so we had to wade the river. I stripped and stood on the bank, gazing at the dirty water rushing past me. A continuous rumble came from the heavy boulders being carried downstream. Fifty feet above me, Frank had wedged himself among some rocks and held the end of the lifeline which I had tied round my waist. It was impossible for either of us to make himself heard above the roar of the water.

I lowered myself into the stream and at once the current nearly carried me away. Before I had gone 3 yards, my feet were numb with cold. One more step and the water was up to my waist, tearing at me. I staggered and gestured wildly to Frank. "Pull on the rope!" I yelled, but he misunderstood and slackened it.

Somehow, I managed to keep my balance and reach dry land again. But that solved none of our problems, for we were still on the wrong side of the river. Three hours' march brought us to a place further up the valley where we could cross by a snow-bridge. After an uncomfortable night on bare rock we headed for a mountain which we later called M10, for from its summit we hoped to get a good view of Mulkila and its neighbours.

But Frank soon found the climbing too strenuous, as his scientific work had left him no time to get into proper training. When I suggested I should climb M10 alone, he gladly consented, though it meant waiting on a bare spur of rock all day until I returned. I did not, incidentally, reach the top that day.

"Did you find any insects?" I asked when I rejoined him in the evening.

"Insects? I've found one grasshopper." He sounded rather melancholy, but added, evidently as a matter of interest: "It has no wings."

Grasshoppers? Wings? Did I know they had wings? Well – yes and no.

It was almost midnight when we reached our tents, dead tired and a little disgruntled by a state of affairs that, after all, was by no means new: this man went too fast for that man, and that man was too slow for this.

* * * *

Next day, Ludwig, Johnny, Hilda and Donald arrived punctually at the mission house in Kyelang with two Sherpas, by name Ang Tsering and Ang Babu. Our third Sherpa had fallen ill and been left in the hospital at Kulu; otherwise, the journey had been uneventful. On the last stage before Kyelang, all six of them had crossed the 15,000-foot high Rangcha Gali Pass to get a panoramic view of the mountains. They had brought five muleloads of food and equipment with them.

It was August 25, 1939. I asked Ludwig about the international situation. "There is little change since you left Vienna," he said. "But people still think there is a war coming."

I gathered that the Scots Commissioner of Police in Dharmshala had been none too kind to Ludwig. After keeping him waiting a long time, he had told him that he was only letting him through to Lahul because he was with three English people.

To offset this gloomy news, Ludwig had brought some mail with him. First, there was a letter from my wife, who was already in England working on the farm owned by a man whom she had taught to ski in the Tyrol and who was now teaching her to plough. Then my father wrote from Vienna: "Don't take on too much, dear boy – you're no longer a youngster" – which was true in one sense, but not in another. There was also a card from my revered friend, Professor Lammer. I had written to him from Port Said. He replied: "Amazing news! The Himalayas! I dreamt of them once. If the monsoons allow and you can afford as many reliable porters as you need, what's to stop experienced Alpinists like yourselves from bagging a couple of 20,000-footers? The weaker brethren can stay at the base camp or climb passes and take photographs. Fare you well and may you all return safely home, victorious and uplifted."

Though he had tried to sound encouraging, Professor Lammer had put his finger on the weak spot in our expedition. Of our four British companions, only Hilda Richmond possessed much experience of Alpine climbing. She belonged to a British mountaineering club, had studied her "Young" – the most popular climbing handbook published in English[2] – and had given Ludwig and me proof of her excellent climbing technique two years before on the Meije and the Barre des Ecrins. All the same, she was a woman and a very delicate one, and the Himalayas demand stamina as well as technique.

Hilda was the only one of the newcomers whom I had met before. Johnny, who was sitting beside her on that first evening in the mission house, told me he had only done ski-ing before. Being no great talker, he did not divulge until much later on, and then only accidentally, that he had toughened himself for the Himalayas by doing physical jerks for hours each day on the grassy swards of England. Somehow the thought was amusing,

[2] *Mountain Craft* by Geoffrey Winthrop Young. Also, *On High Hills* by the same author. *Translator.*

but living at home and with only moderate means, what else could an Englishman do? Even an impecunious Austrian like myself had been reduced to similar methods. Though there were plenty of mountains for me to climb in preparation for the Himalayas, I could not afford the railway fare to reach them – or rather, it had to be saved for the Great Occasion – and to strengthen my ankles I had walked barefoot to and from school for three hours each day over the steepest hill slopes I could find.

But I was least happy of all about the handsome youth standing on the far side of Hilda, imperturbably sucking his pipe: Don Comber. I have already said that he stepped in at the last moment, and glad indeed we were that he did, otherwise we could never have footed the bill and we would never have set eyes on the Himalayas. Don, on the other hand, had never even seen the Alps. All the same, Ludwig and I were firmly resolved to spare no trouble in opening the way to the peaks for our British companions and, bearing in mind that the ultimate responsibility for their safety was ours, in helping them to share in our own climbing adventures, thereby making some return for their considerably larger contributions to the cost of the expedition.

Exactly a week after my unsuccessful attempt to wade the River Milang, Johnny, Ang Tsering and I made a long night march to the snow-bridge where we crossed the river and then, on the other side, walked all the way back to our starting-point in readiness to build a rope-bridge at dawn. When our friends duly appeared on the opposite bank at first light, a bag with a lump of rock in it was tied to one end of a thin cord and thrown over to them. Attached to the cord we then pulled back a half-inch rope and later one of ⅜-inch diameter. The thicker became the load-bearing rope and the other, the draw-rope and safety-line. On the opposite bank, they managed to tie their end to a tall rock, but on ours the land was flat and we had to build a cairn of heavy boulders. The Reverend Peter, who was something of a black-smith, had supplied us with a purchase block and the first load was now suspended from the hook. Frank was in charge of the operation and stationed himself on top of the rock, while the other Sahibs and twenty good men and true from Sumdo, who were going to carry our equipment to the Base Camp, milled about below him. When the first heavy sack came gliding over to us, the Lahulis yelled with joy and flung their caps in the air. As soon as all the equipment was across, a sheep was hooked on as the first live passenger, then one of the porters came over, and then it was Ludwig's turn.

When its burden was half-way across, the rope broke; Ludwig vanished in the surge, came up again with eyes tight shut, struggled frenziedly as the flood tore past and over him, and then clung for a few seconds to the thin draw-line while Johnny and I heaved with all our might. Ang Tsering took my place and I hastened to the rescue. A few steps into the water and I had Ludwig firmly under the arms. He was pale, and bleeding where the torrent had dashed his head against a rock.

When they saw Ludwig was safe, our friends on the far bank hastily unrigged what remained of the rope-bridge and then set off mutely on a six-hour trek to the more reliable crossing provided by the snow-bridge.

Why had the rope broken? The load-bearing rope had sagged considerably under Ludwig's weight and before Frank could stop them, the porters – ten men or more – had given an almighty heave to prevent the Bara Sahib getting wet!

Thereafter the transport of our equipment further upriver was neither pleasant nor easy, but with a lot of sweat and swearing, the crown of success was finally ours, and late that night we were all at the spot where we intended to set up our Base Camp.

The camp had been set up by tired people in gathering darkness and in the light of the following dawn it looked somewhat peculiar. Sagging tents were dotted about haphazardly. Sacks, cans of paraffin, crates and anonymous bundles littered the ground. A sheep tethered to a stake had tied itself neatly into a parcel. From somewhere beneath the chaos came the sound of snoring. The sun glared.

Then someone stirred, grunted, yawned, and soon, throughout the camp, there was a drone of sleepy talk. "Turn out!" shouted a voice, but everyone remained obstinately turned in, enjoying a last few minutes of warmth in a quilted sleeping-bag, waiting for the roar of the Primus. When that came, the sleepers emerged, unwashed and unshaven, of course, because officially they had only just woken up. At last, a splendid sight, the Bara Sahib came striding from his tent, turbanned like a pagan warrior, but with head wound surely well on the mend, for he carried his camera. A moment later, when Shankr called to breakfast, the muster was complete.

The rope bridge. Frank was in charge of the operation and stationed himself on top of
the rock, while the other Sahibs and twenty good men and true from Sumdo milled
around him *(Ludwig Krenek)*

After breakfast the porters were paid. I already knew most of
them by name. Each received his due from the privy cash and,
more valuable to him, odds and ends which we would otherwise
have thrown away – empty food tins, cardboard cartons, lengths
of leather strap, rope or wire. On the previous day when we had
been crossing the glacier, one young lad had lost his straw
sandals. Finely woven in decorative colours, they were a
treasured possession and he had wept bitterly as he watched the
glacier stream carry them away. Now, as we gave him a pair of
white gym shoes, he wept again, for joy. Then everyone wanted
white gym shoes, but with the best will in the world, we could
not oblige.

We spent the next two days organising the Base Camp, then
we set about getting into training, at the same time reconnoitring

the approaches to the highest mountains in the region. The porters had already gone back to Sumdo; Teschi, the most experienced, having been given a number of stones and told to throw away one each day. When the last had gone, he was to take six men and come up to the Base Camp again. At the same time, an enterprising young man named Nauang was appointed post-runner, linking us with Kyelang.

We were hard on ourselves, so that three climbs were enough to get us into form. To save time, two of them were done concurrently, in two groups. Ludwig took Frank and Don, with Ang Babu as porter, up to the 18,800-foot peak of M10 – a climb which presented no difficulties – and from there took a panorama photograph which we needed for our subsequent sketch-map, while I, with Johnny and Hilda, climbed M10. From the side we approached it, we found very steep ice near the top. Ang Tsering helped us carry our kit as far as the starting-point. The 19,200 feet gave us some trouble, Hilda, particularly, gasping for air, so all the greater was our pride in reaching the summit. But more important still was the sketch we were able to make during the ascent showing the approaches to the three highest mountains – Mulkila, M6 and M7. They were the main objectives of our expedition and could now be attacked.

September 3, 1939. Ang Nima, our third Sherpa, had recovered and come up to the Base Camp with Nauang, the runner, just when we needed him. It was not easy to plan our next move. Frank and Don would have to start their return journey in a week to ten days' time, as their leave ended a fortnight earlier than the others', but we could not split into two parties of three and climb two mountains at the same time, as we had too few Sherpas, apart from the fact that each of us Austrians would have had to look after two of our less-experienced British friends. So we decided to do without porters on the last stages of the climbs so that they could be available for bringing up supplies, and arranged that Ludwig and I should attack Mulkila first, taking Johnny and Don, and then the second highest mountain in Lahul, which we took to be M6, with Hilda and Frank.

The approach to these, the two main objectives of our expedition, led up a southerly branch of the Milang Glacier to a second branch where we intended to establish Camp I. From there, the left-hand side of the glacier would lead us to Mulkila and its neighbour, M6, while from the right we could reach two other high mountains, M7 and M8. (See map on page 11.)

I should mention that it was only later, when we came to drawing a map, that we identified these unnamed mountains by the dull method of allotting them letters and numbers. At the time, we had our own names for them, but these would have looked out of place in Himalayan literature. What use, for instance, would it have been to posterity to be told that Ludwig christened one 20,000-foot mountain "The Savage", that we called "Mr Snowdrop", and another mountain "Richmond Peak"? In fact, only Mulkila already had a native name, so we decided to follow the British precedent of lettering the valleys and giving the mountains nearest to each the corresponding letter followed by a number. According to this system, the second highest mountain in the world after Everest was known as K2.

My sketch-map showed that two more camps were needed beyond Camp I, the first on the approach to Mulkila and the second on M6. We sited them on paper and then worked out a traffic plan between them and the Base Camp. We decided that all those not actively climbing would be required for bringing up food and equipment.

At 7.30 a.m. on September 4, 1939, we set off in fine weather to establish Camp I. Only Shankr Singh remained behind at the Base Camp. We had to cover a distance of nearly five miles and climb 2,500 feet, the site chosen for Camp I being at 16,830 feet. The first and the last parts of the climb would be straightforward going over level portions of the Milang Glacier, but the middle section consisted of an ice-fall, that is, a jumble of *séracs*[3] and crevasses, and before plunging into battle with this obstacle we halted in the shadow of massive ice-walls for a short rest. In early summer, when the glacier was covered with deep snow, it might have been quite easy to find a way through the labyrinth, but in autumn the crevasses gaped and hardly a snow-bridge was left.

Soon we were in the thick of the ice-fall. We made good progress for a while and I felt very pleased with myself for recognizing the various moraines and ice-pools which I had carefully

---

[3] The ice-rubble intersected with crevasses which is sometimes formed when a glacier breaks up on a steep slope.*Translator.*

studied three days previously from M10, and which I had memorized as signposts. But then we faced the worst part of the ice-fall where not even my bird's-eye view had shown me a way through the rents and rifts. Here, the glacier was bare of snow. In front of us and behind, crevasses yawned, their base hidden in opaque blue shadow, while above, a mile-wide wall of ice went rearing skyward.

Johnny and I searched for a way through this obstacle; we were close to the left edge of the glacier and there, if anywhere, we hoped to find it. Hopping and slithering along the crazily distorted ice-wall, we worked towards the lateral moraine until suddenly, by different routes, we came to an area where the broken ice had been compressed and lay partly hidden under rubble. Meanwhile, we had been forced down a little and had tried several times to climb up again, each at a different spot, but without success.

Beyond the narrow band of the moraine, wide crevasses again appeared at right angles to the main sweep of the glacier, and the ice had become twisted into fantastic towers and pinnacles. Here, I was certain, lay our only hope of getting through.

Johnny had emerged from the ice-wall higher up than I had and now he saw he was on the right track he went into a kind of quickstep, probably evolved as a finale to his training on the lawns of England! I can picture him now, a little black figure hopping and scrambling hither and thither with demoniac energy over the dully gleaming ice, gradually dwindling as he climbed higher and higher. Sometimes he would vanish for a few moments in a chasm, then emerge at another point, then stop, probably at a crevasse, and come down to get round it, then go scrambling up again with redoubled fury. At last I heard a shout of triumph: Johnny was through; the rest of the glacier was easy going.

An hour later, all of us were through the gap with our heavy loads. From now on, the glacier was completely flat and deep in snow. We could see the tracks of an ibex leading towards the island of rock where we intended to set up Camp I, and, following them, the huge cat's paws of a snow leopard. We reached our goal at 2 p.m., six and a half hours after leaving the Base Camp. We collapsed, exhausted, on the bare rock and not a few of us felt distinctly sorry for ourselves as our fingers explored the gashes where the pack straps had cut into our shoulders.

The sunlight on the snow was so brilliant that even through dark glasses it hurt the eyes. And yet it was not warm. Dominating the south arm of the Milang Glacier, where it surged out from behind a towering wilderness of rock, were two 20,000-foot peaks with really fearsome looking ice-walls. These were only a short distance from us and we gazed at them with awe. Mulkila was invisible.

After a short rest, Frank and Hilda had to return to the Base Camp with the Sherpas, while Don, Johnny, Ludwig and I remained behind amidst the others' artistically scattered equipment. From these heaped objects, Camp I had somehow to take shape. First, we cleared the loose boulders from the rocks above us; then we made level platforms of rubble for the two tents. We could make do with the larger tent for the first night, but next morning the Sherpas were due to bring up more supplies and sleep at the camp. Time passed quickly and in a matter of minutes, it seemed, the cookers were humming their evensong.

The Compur shutter of Ludwig's camera was sticking and it fell to me to take it completely to pieces, clean it and put it together again. I had no knowledge of such things and my only tool was a pocket knife. With cold fingers, the work needed some patience. I sat down in the entrance to the tent, and soon minute screws and springs were strewn around me, each in its special little place. Clearly, whatever happened, no one could go into the tent until I had finished. At last, after opening up and closing down, and unscrewing and screwing, I had done it. Ludwig took the camera, tested it, and to his speechless joy, found that the shutter was now working properly. Then: "Ah! I nearly forget!" he said. "One very important point – did you remember to screw in the outer lens to exactly the right distance? If not, the pictures will be out of focus." So once again, I unscrewed, Ludwig examined, found all well, or made some adjustment – I cannot remember which – and then, by Saint Christopher!, for the last time – spit on the knife-blade, stick the little screw to it, move it slowly, slowly over, take aim and – plop! Hurrah! – straight into the hole. Now turn, gently, until the thread of the screw engages, then tightens, and – finished! Immediately, there was a stampede and in charged the frozen populace with steaming soup-bowls.

Much, much later, when the expedition was long past, Ludwig discovered that the lens had not been in quite the right place, after all; and, hidden in a fold of my wallet, I discovered two little black paper washers – for excluding light from the camera.

* * * *

To me, the following day was among the most enjoyable of the whole expedition. To start with, we hiked, as comfortably as at home on the Dachstein, but amidst unforgettable Himalayan scenery. Then came some brisk work, tackling ice and rock, as a result of which we knew for certain we could at any rate get as far up Mulkila as the final ramparts, which lay at about 20,000 feet.

Ludwig, Johnny, Don and I were the first men to penetrate the wild region which I had selected from M10 as our starting-point for Mulkila. Though leading the file, I cannot claim to have felt the solemnity of the occasion, for I was busy sizing up the glittering ice-wall of a mountain to our right, which we christened "Lyskamm", and to left, the head of a glacier, just coming into view, with Mulkila and its long southerly escarpment rearing inhospitably above the snow basin. But my chief preoccupation was the route we had mapped for ourselves over a grim wall of rock leading up to the saddle between the two mountains.

We reached the level snow at the head of the glacier almost exactly at midday and halted to consider Mulkila at close quarters. There were two main obstacles to be tackled: the wall of rock and ice leading up to the saddle between Mulkila and Lyskamm, and the 1,350-foot high flank of the tower-shaped summit of Mulkila itself.

As the wall up to the saddle would clearly be very difficult, we asked Don to stay behind and do nothing but keep an eye on us. There was a choice of two routes: one straight up the crumbling face of the cliff, and the other, over the broken ice in the angle where the side of the Lyskamm joined the south ridge of Mulkila. I would have preferred to climb the ice, but Ludwig strongly favoured the shorter way up the cliff, so we decided to try it.

Once we were on the cliff, the route was indeed a short one. Fifteen to twenty minutes of steep going brought us on to the saddle, and the climb had not even been difficult. But we were horrified to see many loose rocks on the cliff face that sooner or later would inevitably go hurtling down on to the spot where we

Mulkila (21,380 feet) — the main objective of the first expedition — which was successfully climbed on September 7, 1939 *(Ludwig Krenek)*

had been cutting steps and holds for well over an hour in order to reach the rocks. Soon after this climb, I recorded my impressions:

I was in the upper, vertical part of the ice-curtain. One hundred feet below me gaped the *bergschrund*.[4] Slowly and cautiously I wormed my way out of the niche on to a narrow, glass-smooth ledge. One stamp, or even a sudden movement, and it might collapse. I felt it would be better to work quickly, so I started cutting a step in the ice;

---

[4] The gap which opens at the top of a glacier when the ice starts to move downwards. *Translator.*

then a hole for the fingers. Then a brief pause. Using the ice-axe in the left hand was tiring. I slipped my arm through the sling to free my fingers, then raised my left foot and eased it gently into the step. Next, my left hand felt for the hole, and gripped. Then the right hand let go its safe hold on an icicle and came up beside the left, found the hole, and gripped. Now I could let go my left hand and swing the axe again. Chip – chip – chip! The second step ...

When we reached the saddle a new world was revealed. Below us, on the far side, lay a mass of intersecting *firn*[5] fields at the head of a majestic glacier that trailed down towards the Upper Chandra Valley. Opposite us stood a boldly shaped mountain, similar in outline to the Aiguille Blanche de Peuterey. In the distance, Chandra Tal, the Moon Lake, was glittering in the sun, while on the eastern horizon we could see the mountains of Spiti. The whole scene gave an impression of vast space and was harsh in colour and form. We all felt the urge to explore the glacier and we made up our minds to do so as soon as possible. But meanwhile – Mulkila.

To start with, we would have to tackle some rock towers, and then a long steep slope covered with snow. High above this rose the grey-black mass of the peak. It deserved to be treated with respect for two reasons: firstly, because of the steepness of the rock face joining the snow ridge, and secondly, because we could not tell in advance what our physical reactions would be to the altitude.

The Lyskamm (M6) was much nearer and much lower, the ridge rising straight from the saddle, where we were standing, to the first of its two peaks. But this ridge would also prove a hard nut. It bristled with knife-edged ice ridges and treacherous cornices.

Fifteen minutes after reaching the saddle we started the climb down, this time taking the longer way over steep broken ice further to the south. The first obstacle was a wide, flat-bottomed gully of sheer ice which we had to cross. It was very steep, but we could still avoid step-cutting, relying on our excellent crampons. Half-way we drove a long piton into the ice, which gave us safety then and on the two future occasions when we were to pass this point.

---

[5] *Firn*, or *névé*, is the name given to snow at the head of a glacier which is in the process of turning to ice. *Translator.*

The next snag was a very wide and steep ice-chimney partly covered with snow. It brought us a good deal lower. We foregathered again in a shallow basin where the floor sloped slightly outwards and was criss-crossed with irregular crevasses dangerously masked by snow. The walls were of partly overhanging ice.

As we could find nothing easier, we climbed straight down from here over very steep curtains of ice to our rendezvous with Don. All went well, but being last on the rope, I felt the steepness particularly, and realized that after climbing Mulkila we should have to cut a great many steps if our tired legs were to get us safely down.

The descent took two and three-quarter hours, exactly the same time as the ascent. We found the Sherpas waiting for us on the island of red rock where we had sited Camp I. Frank and Hilda had loaded them with full rucksacks and then they had come up alone over the ice-fall. We had asked the Himalayan Club to send us experienced porters and they had done so. Ang Tsering was the only surviving witness of the tragedy on Nanga Parbat in 1934, when Willo Welzenbach, Ulrich Wieland, Willy Merkl and six Sherpas had lost their lives. After four days of continuous snow-storms Ang Tsering had reached Camp IV with the terrible news; he was badly frost-bitten and had been assumed lost with the others. Ang Nima and Ang Babu had been on Everest, Kangchenjunga and in the Garhwal Himalayas.

That our ever-cheerful Nepalese could negotiate the difficult glacier stretches alone simplified everything immensely. But the praises of the Sherpas have been sung often enough, and there is no need for me to repeat them here. As regards their climbing abilities, the three performed like apt beginners. With us they learned how to use crampons and brushed up their knowledge of rope-work. Ang Tsering surpassed the other two in organising ability and in pathfinding, but, probably as a result of his Nanga Parbat experiences in 1934, he was less certain than they when on steep climbs. All three men were eager for knowledge and could speak some garbled English, but none could read or write. It was really amusing to watch them at the Base Camp dictating letters home in Nepalese while the cook, who understood not one word of what they were saying, wrote down the sounds phonetically in the Devangari script. Heaven alone knows what the recipients made of the result.

Our reconnaissance of Mulkila had taken place on September 5, 1939. Next day, in less than four hours, we and the three porters climbed to the place where Don had waited for us and set up two two-man tents there. We would have preferred a higher site for the camp, as the 2,500 feet of difficult climbing which lay between it and the summit was rather a lot for mountaineers who had had so little opportunity of getting acclimatized. But, with their heavy loads, it would have been impossible for the porters to scale the steep wall up to the saddle and we did not feel inclined to try hauling up the tents ourselves.

So the Sherpas climbed down to Camp I again and, later in the day, to the Base Camp, while the four of us – Ludwig, Johnny, Don and I – spent the rest of the day doing nothing. After snowing for a couple of hours, it cleared towards evening and we crept into our sleeping-bags with eager hopes of the morrow.

Next morning, September 7, before setting off on our attempt to climb Mulkila, I suffered a temporary relapse into the long-forgotten Anglophobia of my boyhood years. Dear Johnny, dear Don, forgive me! You could not guess what agonies of impatience I endured while you cooked and ate your English breakfast, and I think Ludwig felt the same. Though I had woken you at three o'clock, it was 5 a.m. before we set off.

Don went ahead with me, Ludwig and Johnny following as the second rope team. The sky had been clear at dawn, but now there were one or two clouds about and a sharp wind whipped the freshly fallen snow into our faces. I had worked out a route which, though longer even than the way we had come down, would spare us the steep ice-walls below the shallow basin. The chimney gave us little trouble, but crossing the gully took up a lot of time. Don, as a novice, had to be specially looked after, and the cold made us all stiff and clumsy. Negotiating the cliff under the saddle was also rather harder for four than for three, and so it was 7.30 before we reached the ridge, two and a half hours after we had left camp. We then rested for half an hour.

Shreds of mist and cloud were trailing over the ranges and there was no heat in the sun. On our feet once more and facing Mulkila, we saw that some rock towers would be our first obstacle. Ludwig and Johnny took over the lead, heading left towards some faults in the rock. Beyond them, the steep snow-covered shoulder began. The *firn* was hard, so we needed crampons, but could do without the rope and that gave Johnny a chance to get some distance ahead. Ludwig was busy with his camera while I was doing my best to keep Don in good shape, the two of us climbing on slowly after the others and stopping at regular intervals. Don was suffering badly from the height and I was none too happy during this monotonous part of the climb. After two hours, we reached a spur of rock where Johnny had been waiting for us for some time. From there on, the ridge widened until, at the far end which was still a long way off, the southern buttress of the mountain rose steep and bare to the summit.

We had half an hour's rest, but at the end of it Don was feeling no better. Realising that we were short of time and that he was slowing down the rest of us, he generously offered to wait while Ludwig, Johnny and I went on to the summit. So, shortly before 11 a.m. we left Don sitting on the spur of rock at a height of 19,700 feet.

The three of us now went all out for the summit. The snow-ridge continued to offer no real difficulties, but fissures and cornices combined to give us plenty of excitement, and that is always a great help against mountain sickness. Within the hour, we had reached the end of the ridge and the final cone was rearing menacingly above us. While we were taking off our crampons, I had time to inspect the black wall of rock. It was as though one of the smaller peaks in the Dolomites had been planted here on top of the ridge, bearing in mind that the ridge itself was at 20,000 feet. Though much of the rock was almost vertical, I could see some gullies, chimneys and ledges which offered a possible route.

After some perilous climbing on sharp-pointed rock towers, we reached the foot of the main wall. There was just room enough for the three of us to stand if we kept close together. The wall began with a perpendicular section about fifty feet high. Eight feet above us we could see the start of a narrow ledge leading round a corner to our right.

Now came Ludwig's great moment: he was to lead us to the summit. He started to climb. The first 8 feet were difficult. Now he was on the ledge, standing, with smooth walls of rock immediately overhead. Now he was edging along to the right, towards the corner. The rock was overhanging slightly and forcing him out and the holds were uncertain. He was climbing slowly, husbanding his energies because of the altitude. Now he was out of sight round the corner, on the right-hand wall. The rope jerked along inch by inch. Finally it stopped. We shouted, but the words were lost in the wind droning over the ridge.

Johnny, as second man, was belaying our leader, so I could risk climbing out further down to the right to get a view of Ludwig. So that was it! The ledge had come to an end. The wall above him offered a few holds, but it was vertical and before tackling it I felt we ought to make sure there was no easier route.

"Come back! We'll try the other side!"

As experienced mountaineers know, getting back after a difficult climb is often an exhausting business. Ludwig performed well, but by the time he reached us, he was puffing and blowing. Johnny and I offered to take his place, but he would not hear of it, and after a brief rest, he started to climb up the left-hand face. Here the going was easier. A ledge led him right away from the edge, but downwards slightly and if there had been an alternative, we would have taken it. But we could see no weak spot in the wall above us, so we had to keep following the ledge, even when we lost height still further.

At last, we found two parallel fissures running steeply upwards. Ludwig made his choice and, squeezing into a cleft, started to work his way up. It was difficult climbing, but nothing exceptional and eventually we all got through. From here on, gullies alternated with shelves covered with debris and the going was easier. We came to a small trough surrounded by brightly coloured rock pinnacles. An easily negotiable chimney led us through a gap shaped like a gateway, then followed some awkward traversing of slabs and then a long gully in loose rock. The gully emerged on to a talus slope.[6] Above it glittered the snow-capped summit. There would be no more obstacles. Victory was in our grasp.

We congratulated Ludwig and then, because the tension had slackened, he suddenly began to feel the height. It was now 21,300 feet. "You go on," he said. "I'll follow slowly." But of course we would not allow it. We unhitched the rope and, with

---

[6] Consists of a mass of boulders and rubble which has been loosened by weathering and has rolled down the mountainside. Often, a slight movement is enough to set the whole mass in motion again. *Translator.*

Ludwig still leading, climbed cautiously up the talus slope. I was having less difficulty in breathing than the others, hence I carried the rope. Strangely enough, I had felt the height much worse 3,000 feet lower down.

Slowly we approached the snow-cap and once there, we were soon on the summit. We reached it at 2.10 p.m., eight and a half hours after leaving camp. The climb up the summit cone had taken us two and a half hours. Now we were at a height of 21,380 feet and had achieved the main objective of our expedition. And the date was September 7,1939. In Europe, the first week of the second World War was just coming to an end.

Perhaps the reader is expecting me to describe what we saw from the highest point in Lahul, but unfortunately we saw practically nothing, although we stayed on top for a whole hour. There was cloud when we reached the summit, and cloud when we left. We collected some small pieces of rock, read the barometer, took the temperature (30°F.) and entered the figures in our note-book. Then we ate up the remains of our food. For some time we lay resting on a patch of scree, but the fear we should miss something kept driving us to our feet to climb on top of the snow-drift at the highest point, alas, to see the same unvarying blanket of grey cloud. Once, for a brief moment, we glimpsed the outline of the giant neighbours of our peak, and Johnny quickly aligned his water-level, which he had made of two glass tubes and a length of rubber pipe. There was no doubt that Mulkila was the highest point.

Before leaving the summit at 3.10 p.m., we built a cairn of stones and put a tin can inside with the date of our climb. Then we started the descent, fully realising that we would have a race against time. We had a long and difficult route to cover before reaching our tents and by 7 p.m. it would already be getting dark.

So that we would find our way on the return, Johnny and I had set up a number of cairns and I had, as well, taken careful note of some of the salient features. It was now a real pleasure to lead the party down quickly and unerringly over the complicated terrain to the point where we had left our crampons. From there, we hurried down to Don, who congratulated us and gave us food which he had saved from his own rations.

Frank's experiences when waiting for my return from M10 had taught me that, far from reviving one's energies, a long rest at an unaccustomed altitude merely stiffens the limbs and tires the body, and so it was with Don. Ludwig now took him on the rope while Johnny and I had the more congenial task of hurrying ahead to cut steps diagonally across the broad ice-gully below the saddle, thus saving them a good deal of time. I remember us speeding down the ice-slopes in carefree style and taking the rock-towers in our stride for the sheer fun of clambering over them. True, we had then to cope with the ice-wall and its very considerable difficulties and, in the event, we were held up long enough for Ludwig and Don to catch up with us.

We manfully worked our way down the great ice-wall, without noticing at first that the daylight was beginning to fade, and when we did, the urge to go faster fought with the need for great care. As long as the old, thick *firn* was covering the ice, the axe could be driven in deep and the first man on the rope encouraged to move fast. But with fresh snow lying sticky and slippery on the ice, we had to climb down cautiously, one step at a time. By one rope's length after another, Johnny and I tapped our way down, and still there was no end to the slopes and they seemed almost as steep as ever. Above our heads we could hear Ludwig and Don working in the ice, but could not see them.

It was completely dark by the time the slope began to flatten out, and our next problem was to find the tents. But we had maintained direction well and we came straight to them. By 7.30 p.m. we were all back and under cover, and the great climb was over.

*   *   *   *

The next day brought fine weather, a day too late for the Mulkila party. We did not stir from the tents until we could feel the heat of the sun through the canvas; then we celebrated with a leisurely breakfast and lashings of tea.

When climbing up to the south ridge on Mulkila we had seen that Lyskamm (M6), which we had taken to be the second highest mountain in the group, was in fact considerably lower than M7, one of the mountains bordering the south Milang Glacier, and consequently we had to make a radical change of plan. We could no longer start our second expedition from the camp where we now were, but would have to set up another on the southern arm of the glacier. This involved taking all our equipment down to Camp I, and for that we needed the Sherpas.

So while I stayed with the tents, Ludwig, Johnny and Don went down to send three Sherpas up to me. A few hours later, they arrived, reserved, polite and willing as ever. After I had made tea for them and given them something to eat, the four of us made up a rope-team and trotted comfortably down the lovely route to Camp I. There I had a joyful reunion with Hilda, who was feeling in good form for the attempt on M7, and with Frank, my bearded companion on previous adventures. He, too, was full of confidence and it was a real pleasure to be with him again. Johnny and Don had already gone further down to the Base Camp. On them now fell the responsibility for sending up further supplies.

On September 9, 1939, Ludwig, Frank, Hilda and I with the three Sherpas started up the south arm of the Milang Glacier. The scenery was superb. On our left, a tongue of the glacier lolled in blue ice-waves between huge red pillars of rock. From this angle, Lyskamm revealed a massive granite flank, while M7, our objective, showed us a positively frightening ice-wall scoured by avalanches and lined with gullies dug by melted ice. At the sight, Ang Nima came to a standstill and said thoughtfully: "Sahib! Here, it look like on Kangchenjunga."

The wall below the lowest point of the ridge between M6 and M7 looked steep and unapproachable, so we began to climb further to the right, where we hoped to find room for our tents in a snowed-up cleft below the ridge. The slopes were becoming steeper and we put on crampons. Hilda and Frank were performing extremely well, and the porters worked their way up and over the ice with skill and courage. Finally, we reached a crevasse beyond which an even steeper slope led up to the site we had chosen for our camp.

Here the party rested, while I climbed up to the snow-covered cleft, finding, as we had hoped, that there was room for our tents. But on the way I met something that made my flesh creep: a whole network of broad and probably bottomless crevasses covered by a paper-thin crust of ice. I must have looked shaken when I got back, for the others insisted on my swallowing a few mouthfuls of food before I roped to lead them up to the campsite. It was 1 p.m. when we got there. As the Sherpas had to return to Camp I, I set off at once to lead them down again over the last steep buttress. On the far side of the crevasse, I told them once more what they had to do. Ang Tsering and Ang Babu were to return to us at noon on the following day. Ang Nima was to go back to the Base Camp. Then I wished them a good trip and for the third time crept back alone over the crevasses with their treacherous, transparent roofs.

Meanwhile, my friends had been busy. The platforms were almost finished and soon the tents were up, with the openings facing each other and a small space between covered with a ground-sheet to keep off the snow. Ever since our arrival it had been snowing as in mid-winter and all we could see of M7 through the whirling flakes were shimmering ice-slopes and its imposing outline. But we needed no further inspection to know that M7 would be no easy mountain to climb. To our left towered the rocky mass of M6, Lyskamm, part black, part yellowish red, and now becoming dappled by the great flakes falling slowly in the still air. Behind was a blue overhanging ice-shelf and above it, an ice-buttress with a thickening mantle of snow merging into the grey sky. At our feet, the ice plunged deep into a steel-blue snowing void, and beyond that – far distant and invisible – lay the world of men.

Our instruments showed a height of 19,200 feet and a temperature of 29°F.

At 2 a.m., when I looked at the weather, it was still snowing heavily. At 3 a.m. – no change. At 4 a.m. – still no change. In such weather, one had to pluck up courage to leave the warmth of the tent and go outside: there were boots to put on and take off, snow to be scraped from clothing, and frenzied contortions were needed to get back into one's sleeping-bag. These were serious deterrents, but there were tines when they weighed little against other, more urgent, considerations, and at one such moment, some hours later, I noticed that the sky was clearing. There were great gaps in the seamless grey pall and as the clouds jostled their way out of the valley, a splendid wintry scene was revealed, the mountains standing, austere and silent in their snowy mantles, around the spotless white of the glacier. For a few seconds I was spellbound. Then I roused the others. The time was 7.30 a.m.

Despite the late hour we decided to make an attempt on M7 as we were no more than 1,600 feet below the summit, though a longish ridge with two humps lay between us and the saddle whence the mountain reared steeply, with its summit lost in cloud. The weather had not cleared completely after all, though at least it had stopped snowing. Ludwig and Hilda hacked their way up the ice, Frank and I following them. After a few rope-lengths we reached the ridge, then turned right towards our objective. The going now became very rough, as the *firn* had formed into pinnacles, or *pénitentes*, as the South Americans call them. Where rock appeared it was reasonably tame, though always covered with ice or fresh snow. The two humps on the ridge turned out to be sizeable peaks. The climb proved nowhere really difficult, but it was arduous throughout and the grey mist depressed our spirits. By 10 a.m. we were at the true foot of our mountain and facing the hardest part of the climb. We were by no means sure that we wanted to go on.

It is tempting in such a situation to have a long rest and plenty to eat. We succumbed to both these temptations, but in the end, the weather was still uncertain. Clouds were still trailing about; behind us, mist was rising from the valley of the glacier and only occasionally an anaemic sun peered from the cheerless autumn sky. Through gaps in the mist, we could see our tents on the ice-slope. We had come a good way from them, but only a little higher.

Leading up to the mountain itself was a steep *arête* covered with *firn*, with its highest point resting against the steep, icy flank of a shoulder crowned with rocks. It looked as if we could reach the summit from the shoulder by a ridge with a somewhat gentler slope, where we would be unlikely to meet serious snags. The worst part of the climb would undoubtedly be the *arête* and the steep wall of granular snow and ice leading from it to the shoulder. All this we deduced from glimpses obtained on the previous day and from what we could now observe, for the summit of M7 was still shrouded in mist and cloud.

Towards midday the weather began to look more friendly and we started to attack the ice-wall, Ludwig and Hilda leading. When climbing on steep rock, the mountaineer never knows till the last moment whether he is going to get through or not, but on a normal ice-wall the possibility of reaching the top is never in doubt. On the other hand, there is the constant danger of slipping and falling which increases with each step the climber takes, particularly when the highest part of the wall is also the steepest. Ice-walls are a test of nerves and M7 was no exception.

But our crampons held marvellously in the ice, and Ludwig only needed to cut steps every fifteen yards, big ones in which we could stand with both feet and belay the rope. Near the top, the ice-wall became very steep, but Ludwig worked quickly and steadily and Hilda had no difficulty in following him.

On the shoulder we were met by a biting wind. Mist was seething up from the valley, hiding most of the grim wall between us and the Milang Glacier. The summit of M7 was now well and truly lost in cloud, and as it was very late and we were a long way from camp as well, there was talk of turning back.

"Let's keep on climbing until two," I suggested. "Whatever happens then, we'll turn back, even if we haven't reached the summit." No one raised any objections, so I took over the lead with Frank and began to make what use I could of the reprieve. For some reason, I was convinced that M7 would not elude us and, instead of walking up the shoulder, whenever Frank stopped to pay out the rope it seemed the most natural thing in the world to run. But that was not enough. I had to rouse the others for an all-out effort. At first, my encouraging remarks failed to find much of an echo, but the response steadily improved until finally the whole party was scurrying up the slope in true victory mood.

From the shoulder we pressed on along the ridge, meeting rock towers at first which we were able to circumvent. Then came a steep up-gradient of loose rock and, finally, nothing but steep ice covered with fresh snow ready to start sliding at any moment. Further on we met snow pinnacles again and these made the going rather easier. We were beginning to feel the warmth of the sun now through the thick, soupy mist, which meant that we must be nearing its upper limit. The only snag was that the ridge seemed to go on for ever. More and more *pénitentes* kept looming up, their edges suffused with yellow light from the sun which lay hidden in mist behind them. From 3 to 6 feet high, these pinnacles took up the whole ridge in two, sometimes three lines, and where there was space to climb between them the ascent became no more dangerous than going up a flight of stairs between banisters.

Time passed and still we went on climbing. Those behind were becoming less talkative, less eager, I noticed, in their response to my words of good cheer. And, indeed, there was not much cause for joy: the time was now two o'clock and we were all puffing like steam-engines. Then came a gleam of hope. Ahead, another ridge appeared, curving away from us. The summit was not far off: Frank and I pressed aside to let the second rope-team past, then Ludwig stopped and let Hilda go on ahead to surmount the last few yards and be the first to stand on the summit. In her modest way, she tried to refuse, but we insisted, and a few minutes later she was there, and then all of us were shaking hands on the highest point of M7.

But sad to relate, we saw nothing from this proud peak either – nothing but thick, yellow mist. The temperature was below freezing, but we did not feel cold as the sun's rays warmed the mist and the wind had dropped. With great relish we ate a tin of peaches and some biscuits. No one suffered from the altitude and we all felt fresh and strong, despite the tempo we had maintained from the shoulder to the summit. It was a wonderful half-hour.

Apart from a subsidiary peak of Mulkila, M7 is the second highest mountain in Lahul, its height, according to our calculations, being 20,800 feet. We could not discover whether it has a local name, but as it cannot be seen from the surrounding villages, I doubt it. Hence, when drawing our map, we gave it a letter and a number.

The ridge proved harder on the descent. And how we longed to get the ice-wall behind us! But all things come to an end – we worked our way down without a hitch and then along the ridge, with one or two pauses for rest. Through the banked clouds we yodelled down to the tents and the Sherpas replied, yet we still had difficulty in finding them as all our tracks had been wiped out and the mist was thickening. It was not until 5.20 p.m. that we were jumping down, one at a time, from the last steep slope above the tents, to arrive, all four of us, safe and sound.

We were enormously pleased to see the reliability of our Nepalese porters, particularly of Ang Nima, who had come all the way up from the Base Camp that afternoon after covering the same long and arduous route in reverse on the previous day. It took a few minutes only to pack up the tents and sleeping-bags, but then we had to allow ourselves time for food and rest. At 6 p.m. – pretty late – we set off for Camp I. I had three heavily laden porters on my rope and leading them down over the ice-slope below the bivouac and then acting as anchor while they skated over the crevasses was a responsible job. But once that ordeal was over, I could treat them as though they were an experienced rope-team and let them carry on much as they liked, following the still clearly visible tracks which they had made on their ascent.

By the time we reached the pillars of red rock it was dark and Ludwig, Frank and Hilda were some way behind.

I called to Ludwig, "Shall we wait?"

"No!"

The three Sherpas and I started to jog-trot. At first I had been relieved the others had not wanted us to wait, but soon I began to wish they had. My team were crossing this glacier for the fourth time in two days and they felt very much at home. The speed they kept up almost winded me. Ahead, Ang Tsering was zigzagging dizzily, jumping fissures, groping his way over ice-bridges and seldom troubling to think of the three men roped behind him. Two of them were all right, they were kindred spirits. Only myself, at the end of the rope, felt differently. I was just flesh and blood, an ordinary human being, but the Sherpas obviously weren't – they had lynx-eyes and leg muscles of steel. Besides, I had just climbed a high mountain. But pride stifled my protests and kept me going helter-skelter after the others.

Then, further down, Ang Tsering lost the way – it was pitch dark – and we found ourselves in a part of the glacier that was even more broken up. That seemed to drive him stark mad, and when at last we stumbled into Camp I over innumerable runnels which water had dug in the ice, I had more than once been reduced to crawling on hands and knees. But no one was to know that – as I have said, it was dark.

*   *   *   *

The eleventh of September, 1939, began like a winter's day. When we woke up the snow was 4 inches thick and it went on snowing all morning. We lazed until 1 p.m., but then worked quickly, encouraged by a gap in the clouds through which the sun poured down on to the whitest of Himalayan landscapes. Even through snow-glasses, the light was almost blinding. Within an hour we had packed everything and were on our way to the Base Camp.

The sun soon vanished again as swollen clouds, driven by the monsoon, came snaking over the mountain ridges to merge into an opaque grey blanket over the Milang Glacier. The ice-fall gave us some awkward moments. Quite rightly, the Sherpas asked to be roped as the ice was covered with a slippery layer of fresh snow, and with their heavy loads they found it almost impossible to keep their balance. Below the ice-fall, however, we came out of the mist and found ourselves on harmless, snow-free stretches of the glacier where we could do very much as we liked – run, walk, or even stand still and take photographs.

As soon as we were in sight of the Base Camp, Johnny and Don came hurrying out to relieve Hilda of her rucksack. Then – what an evening! – Shankr excelled himself as cook. Johnny and Don, the ever good humoured, ever helpful, ever pipe-sucking Don, took it in turns to keep everyone's plate full; Hilda, needless to say, being the object of special attention. Though he must have felt exhausted, Frank thawed out properly as he told the others of our climb, while before, during and after the meal, Ludwig and I drank cup after cup of hot tea and cocoa.

The Sherpas, too, celebrated with a slap-up dinner. It was they who first saw a light coming up towards us over the glacier. Aren't we lucky, we said. That must be Nauang, the postman, bringing us letters from home. And what luck we'd already had; Everything had gone marvellously well. We had done all we had set out to do. We had all the essential data now for a map of the Milang area. On the journey up, Ludwig and I had managed to do a good deal of preparatory work for our proposed studies on past and recent glaciation. As a zoologist, Frank was content. Hilda was pleased with her botanical finds. As for our mountaineering exploits: in the fortnight we had been in the Himalayas, we had climbed four big mountains, including the two highest in Lahul. And though Frank and Don had to leave next morning for Kulu to get home in time for their university terms, the remaining four of us could look forward to another whole fortnight of wonderful climbing.

Or so we thought. But Nauang brought us a newspaper. It was dated September 4, 1939, and the headline spelled WAR. We spent a bad night.

Next morning, we discussed what to do. By a majority we decided to break off the expedition, but first I was to go down to Kyelang to find out if Italy was in the war. If so, the Mediterranean would be closed to shipping, and Frank and Don would get home too late for the start of term. I was also to try to ensure that Ludwig and I were not forcibly separated from our British friends before we had arranged for the safe keeping of our equipment and photographic films, and had shared out the balance standing to my credit in the bank. Lastly, I had somehow to collect twenty porters in Dartse to move our baggage earlier than planned.

While I prepared for the journey, the others wrote letters home for me to post in Kyelang. By late afternoon, all was ready. Though I was determined to avoid premature arrest in Kyelang, the uncertainty made parting difficult. No one knew whether we were saying good-bye or *au revoir*.

Everyone had shaken hands with me and wished me good luck. Only Hilda made no move. I went up to her.

"Hilda?"

"Yes?"

"I'm going now."

"Oh ... Well ... Good-bye, Friedel. Good-bye ...."

Since we had heard of the war, Hilda had seemed lost.

I went hopping and slithering down the steep moraine and, pausing for breath at the bottom, looked round. Small figures stood waving to me from the top of the hill. I pulled out my handkerchief and waved back. Then I turned and went hurrying down to the middle of the glacier. My eyes smarted and there was a lump in my throat; yet, like everyone else, I had known that war was coming. Why, now that it had come, did it seem such an overwhelming blow?

As I walked down the valley, the scenery offered no novelties to distract my gloomy thoughts. I kept up a good speed and before dark had got the steep drop at the end of the glacier behind me. I found a sheltered spot in a gully where I could spend the night half lying and half sitting. I would have enjoyed a fire, but it was too dark to go looking for twigs and, at any rate, without it nature made a more powerful effect. Above me stood the stars. The two rivers roared. I was exactly at their confluence.

Next morning I was greatly surprised to find I could wade the south branch of the Milang River without taking too much of a risk. Now that the nights were lengthening and getting colder, less snow was melting and the water-level was much lower.

In Sumdo young and old were working in the fields. They all knew me by now and no one treated me as a stranger. Teschi came running up and I told him at once that we needed twenty porters instead of the seven we had earmarked for Frank's and Don's luggage. None of them yet knew of the war.

Slowly the miles to Kyelang dwindled. I had to do a two days' march in one. On reaching the village I waited outside until dark, then crept down the only street to the mission house. I was lucky to find the Rev. F. A. Peter and his sister, Elizabeth, still there. On the outbreak of war they had packed up all their belongings and were now living in empty rooms. They wanted to move to Leh, but had first to get their Society's approval.

While Mr. Peter fixed up a bed for me on the floor, his sister fed me royally. After the meal, I just managed to stay awake long enough to read the newspapers received since the outbreak of war, and gathered that Italy was in no hurry to become a belligerent. I was also relieved to hear from the missionary that there were no police in Kyelang, for in that case Ludwig and I could travel as far as Manali with our British friends.

Knowing what it meant to have to do four days' journey in two days, the missionary tried hard to think how he could make the return easier for me. He would gladly have lent me his horse, but it needed an experienced rider and the only mount I had ever ridden was a wooden one on the merry-go-round in the Prater in Vienna. Finally, he sent his servant with me, for he, too, possessed a horse, a docile, ambling chestnut that took me as far as Dartse.

Though the route skirted precipices, I found riding easy. Later on, two Lahulis on horseback caught up with us and Mr. Peter's servant was rash enough to tell them that the Sahib had never ridden before. The men then tried to unseat me by goading my animal into a brisk canter, but though I felt terrified I tried not to show it and grinned as though it was all a colossal joke.

Against my better judgement, one of the men then persuaded me to ford the River Bhaga at Sumdo-Dartse. I agreed because it would reduce my journey by almost two hours, but I knew I was asking for trouble. The Lahuli rode ahead and my steed followed. There was a steep, rocky slope down to the river and more than once, as the animal's front hoofs dropped suddenly, I thought I was going to somersault over its head. And then, the current! My horse refused to go in at first and the river was so deep in the middle, the water came nearly up to my knees. But we reached the far bank intact, where I had some difficulty in persuading the Lahuli to take the horse I no longer needed back to its owner, who was waiting for it on the other side.

Late that afternoon I reached the place where we had made our rope-bridge over the river. We had arranged that Don should come down with Ang Nima and meet me here so that they could take the information I had gathered back to the Base Camp. I had expected to see them on the far bank and was prepared to throw over a note weighted with a stone. But to my horror, I found them on my own side of the river. They said that, when they had reached it, they had been so pleased to find they could wade it that they had decided to cross, after all. But now, of course, as I knew it would be, the river was swollen with all the glacier ice that had melted during the day and they were stuck, unable to get back.

There was no point in being annoyed, so I accepted the inevitable and spent the rest of the day in pleasant idleness with Don and Ang Nima. Don had a refreshingly simple way of looking at coming events and he succeeded in diverting my thoughts from the tortuous maze they had been pursuing. As for the Sherpa, it seemed no situation could ever find him at a loss. Deft and unobtrusive as ever, he made tea for us, collected wood for a fire and got out our sleeping-bags.

Soon it was twilight and we were sitting, gazing into the crackling flames. Though the war lay aching at the back of our minds, contentment was uppermost. Despite every obstacle, the expedition had been a success – nothing could alter that. We had climbed our mountains and now we felt pleasantly tired.

But alas, on that same evening at the Base Camp, the worst that can befall a mountaineering expedition occurred – a fatal accident.

On September 13, the day after I had left my friends for Kyelang, they had explored the northern branch of the Milang Glacier, the indefatigable Johnny climbing one last mountain, M3, of 19,000 feet. The following day dawned cold and clear – a perfect autumn day. After breakfast, Hilda and Don stayed behind at the camp with the porters and the cook, while Frank, Johnny and Ludwig climbed a short distance above the tents to do whatever pleased them best on this last day that they would be spending in the mountains. Frank collected fossils and insects, Ludwig took photographs, and Johnny climbed. Later, they saw Don and Ang Nima leave to meet me in the valley as we had arranged and, later still, all three climbed down to the tents for lunch. Hilda was not there, but she had often returned late when collecting botanical specimens and they thought nothing of it. They had their meal, and when it was over and there was still no Hilda, Johnny went out on the most likely route to meet her. Two hours passed, and then he came back alone.

At once, a systematic search was organized. For the three remaining hours of daylight, they combed a widening area, but without avail. After dark they took lanterns and searched the whole of the lateral moraine, climbing down into the crevices and calling at intervals, "Hil – da – – !" There was no reply, no sound except the rustle of ice-water somewhere out of sight.

The search continued until about 1 a.m. on the 15th, when the three men were forced to take a short rest. A few hours later, the eighteen Lahuli porters arrived at the Base Camp and at dawn Frank set off with them to comb the whole area again, sending Don and me a note through Nauang which began: "We can't find Hilda. She vanished yesterday. We are searching ...." But by the time Don and I were reading this terrible news, poor Hilda had been found.

It was Frank and the porters who came on her. She was lying at the bottom of a gully with a fractured skull. Nearby were a hand-towel and a jagged lump of rock the size of a large book. It was impossible to tell exactly how Hilda had met her death. But the night of September 13 had been very cold, as it often is when the weather clears up after a bad spell, and the snow-fields feeding the stream by the Base Camp had frozen with the result that when my friends came to it next morning they found no water. After Don and Ang Nima had left the camp, Hilda must have followed the dried water-course upwards until she came to steep rock. When she found no water there, she must have climbed on through the narrow gully where the stream normally flowed, leaving it when she came to smooth, vertical rock for an easier slope of loose boulders nearby. Here she found what she was looking for: a pool of clear water in the rocks. She had the towel with her and presumably she bent over to have a wash. At that moment she must have been struck on the head by a falling rock – perhaps the rock which was found close to her body – and killed instantly.

I pass over the agonies of suspense which Don and I endured while waiting for further news. We waited by the river bank until the afternoon of September 15, when Don's sharp eyes spotted the whole party coming down the glacier towards us. At last, the leading members reached the opposite bank, among them, Ludwig. He threw over a weighted note which confirmed our worst fears: "Hilda found this morning. We have buried her by the Base Camp."

During the afternoon the river had once more swollen alarmingly, and the men had great difficulty in fording it. When Shankr Singh, our cook, emerged from the water, he spoke the one word "Memsahib", and burst into tears. Frank, Johnny and Ludwig were the last to cross the river, linking arms as the Lahulis had done. We marched on until we had crossed the Yotse suspension bridge; then we bivouacked, setting up the tents on the right bank at the foot of the main pier. We paid off the Lahulis. From now on we could use horses and these were obtainable from Yotse, where the inhabitants already knew us, some of them having acted as porters.

The night by the bridge was clear and cold. The mountain stream roared. The camp-fires glowed. We hardly spoke a word. The small jobs that had to be done were performed automatically – we all knew the routine. I was thinking of Hilda, as we all were, and then of Poland, where thousands were dying, some of them, perhaps, friends of mine. Hilda had been our dear companion and friend through all the delights and dangers of the expedition. Hilda had been one of us – we had lost something of ourselves.

And ahead of us lay war – more dying. More victims would be claimed, perhaps, from our little party, or our families. Tonight each of us thought of that. But no one was poor-spirited. We all ate and drank and smoked, and treated each other kindly, sleeping at last as soundly as in childhood days.

*   *   *   *

Little remains to be told. The march to Kyelang was hot and tiring. I was covering this particular stretch for the sixth time. Half-way we were met by a horsed messenger from the postmaster in Kyelang. He had a letter for me:

To Dr. Friedrich Kolb
and Ludwig Krenek, at present in Lahul.

Dharmshala, September 10, 1939.

Dear Sirs,
I must ask you to return to Manali without delay and there report
to the Inspector of Police.
In your own interest I advise you to act on this request, thereby
making more drastic measures to ensure your attendance
unnecessary. You must understand that the British Empire is at
war with Germany and that you are therefore enemy aliens.

The letter was signed by the Scots Commissioner of Police
who had been so friendly to me in Dharmshala.

We stayed in Kyelang a whole day, as there was a lot of writing
to be done and financial calculations to be made. We also wanted
to read the newspapers and the mail that had arrived for us, and
eat – eat potatoes, vegetables and fruit in immoderate quantities.
This time, Mr. Peter and his sister were our guests. They had still
not heard from the Moravian Mission whether they were to move
to Leh and, as the passes would soon be blocked with snow, time
was getting short.

As it was a Sunday, Mr. Peter held a service in the morning for
his small Christian congregation and told them in Lahuli of
Hilda's death. They then prayed for her, in Lahuli and in their
own fashion, but, I am sure, sincerely.

The day passed quickly and I myself was writing letters and
notes on the expedition until after midnight. At 1 a.m. I finished
a long letter to my wife in England and crept through the
deserted alleyways to the post-box, where the mail would be
collected at 6 a.m.

Ludwig, our English friends and myself were in no hurry to
reach Manali, and next day we went no further than Gundla. It
was a brilliant autumn morning when we left Kyelang, bringing
out all the colours in the scenery. As a parting gift, Miss Peter had
given us a sackful of vegetables and fruit from the Mission
garden. In Gundla we spent the afternoon under some willow
trees at the rest-house. In the evening Frank read out the letter he
had composed to Hilda's parents. Before going to sleep we sang
German and English songs.

The following day took us as far as Khoksar. In perfect
weather, Ludwig and Johnny once more climbed up the Rangcha

Gali Pass to photograph the panorama, and next morning Johnny and I climbed Beas Rikhi, a mountain by the Rohtang Pass from where there was also a clear panoramic view.

It is only now, after visiting other parts of the Himalayas, that I can appreciate to the full the peculiar beauty of Lahul. Lying between the rich forests, the paddy fields and orchards of Kulu and the parched Tibetan landscape of the Upper Indus Valley around Leh, Lahul possesses characteristics of both these regions. During the summer months, the Rohtang and Bara Lacha passes are crossed in both directions by a colourful assortment of people. In Patsio, a treeless and uninhabited site where the valley widens above Sumdo, a great annual fair is held, salt and borax being bartered for tea, barley, wool and manufactured goods. Among those attending the fair, the *gaddis* – shepherds and goatherds – are conspicuous in their short, thick woollen coats. The blue-green, strong-smelling grass of Lahul is famous and each year the *gaddis* move their herds from the winter grazing on the southern slopes of the first Himalayan range, over the passes and down to the summer pastures of Lahul.

Compared with other Himalayan giants, the mountains of Lahul are small, but, like a woman's, their charm is independent of size. And they are only part of a landscape which, considered as a whole, with its villages, their inhabitants and their animals, its vegetation, tracks and pathways, is held by those who know them to be among the most beautiful in the whole of the Himalayas.

Ludwig led the porters over the pass while Frank and Don hurried on to Manali to prevent the Indian police prematurely arresting the "enemy aliens". On the following day, September 21, 1939, we cleaned and packed up all our equipment. The field by the *dak* bungalow at Kothi was littered with ropes, sleeping-bags, tent sheets and clothing. As if by accident, the things that emerged from Ang Tsering's rucksack coincided with those he had earmarked for himself. A talkative Indian, whom curiosity had attracted to the scene, told us that for some days past the police had been expecting two Germans from Lahul. Had we seen them, asked the Indian; he himself was on his way to Lahul. We told him he would probably come across the Germans if he set off at once.

Early that afternoon, Ang Nima brought us this note from

Frank: "Get here as quickly as you can. They are already suspicious. Little risk of premature separation."

It was just over six miles from Kothi to Manali. Ludwig had to wait until the pack-horses were loaded; meanwhile, I went on ahead with Johnny. On the way, we met Frank, who had come out to meet us. He gave us the latest news: Russia had invaded Poland from the East.

Not long afterwards, I found myself in the same room of the *dak* bungalow in Manali where, six weeks before, I had written my final notes for Ludwig on the arrangements for the expedition and then, with some relief, had put on my climbing boots. Now, I sat opposite an Inspector of Police, a smiling Sikh with full beard and magnificent turban. Until Ludwig arrived, we drank tea and chatted non-committally. Then a file of papers suddenly appeared on the table and, glancing through the window, I caught the glint of bayonets.

*   *   *   *

So from Manali onwards Ludwig and I were prisoners, though, to start with, no one bothered to underline the fact. During the first night, for instance, we could have got out and away by the back door of the bungalow, as only the front was guarded – if we had had somewhere to go. But on the following evening we were taken before the friendly Commissioner in Dharmshala. He could not help it, I suppose, but he gave us a shock.

"Good evening," he said to our British friends, pointedly ignoring Ludwig and me. "Come inside and have a whisky and soda." The door stayed open, but we two stayed outside. The Scot chatted over the drinks for a minute or two, then we heard him say: "If you will excuse me? I have some business to attend to with those two gentlemen. Perhaps you would like to sit and read the papers?" He then ordered the sentries to take us to his office and, following us in, closed the door behind him.

At once, his tone changed. "Won't you sit down?" he said pleasantly. "Here is your mail. I'm sorry, but I had to read through it. And here are your letters which you wrote home. I have to return them to you because at the moment there is no postal communication with your country." Then we had to fill out the inevitable "Personal Particulars". The moment we were outside his office, the Commissioner resumed his military tone.

Our next stop was the military jail in Lahore. Here we had to say good-bye to our English friends. Then a huge key turned in a massive padlock and we were "in" – for the duration.

We had each been given a ready-printed card to sign, saying that we were prisoners-of-war and that we were well. The cards reached our relatives in Vienna about a year later. On the other hand, a postcard to an aunt in Switzerland which I had stealthily posted an hour previously as we were passing a letter-box was in my father's hands within a week, so that my parents in Vienna did not have to wait twelve months before they knew whether it was the British who had detained me or a crevasse in the Himalayas.

Our stay in the military prison in Lahore was destined to be short, but we were not to know that and we started at once to fight that creeping desperation, that waiting-for-the-end which is the first enemy of prisoners who cannot tell how long their captivity will last. Our room was quite large so we spent the time doing gymnastics. Ludwig, the champion jumper, soon managed to hurdle the whole length of the table, whereas I, despite my longer legs, had to work up to it in stages. On one occasion we were rudely interrupted by our sergeant jailer. "What the * * * * do you think you're up to?" he bawled. "Stand to attention! You're going to be inspected." Thereupon a British officer brought in an Indian Prince wearing military uniform. The news had got about that three weeks only after the outbreak of war, a couple of strange birds had been caught wandering in Lahore. The Prince now wanted to see them. And he was only the first.

From Lahore, we were passed on to the main internment camp at Ahmednagar. This was the collection centre for almost all German-speaking men who were in India, Iraq, Persia or Afghanistan on the outbreak of war. Amongst the prisoners we found three members of the official German Nanga Parbat expedition, as well as two Bavarians who had been in Sikkim with a Swiss companion. The Swiss had been allowed to return home. The Bavarians were in the next barrack and we saw quite a lot of them. One of them, who was a baker by trade, used to warn us: "Don't go telling anybody how cheaply you managed to get out here or next time we will have our allowance cut." But there was to be no next time for him. A few years later, he escaped from the camp and some villagers murdered him for the sake of the money he had on him.

It was the baker who founded the camp climbing club; it had a regular membership of two, himself and myself. The barracks were built of rough stone and we scratched out the mortar from some of the joints so that we could climb up and down the walls. No one seemed to mind. Though not a very interesting pastime, it was certainly difficult, for here, incontestably for once, was the famous "vertical face" of mountaineering reports. A first-floor balcony provided an excellent overhang.

By the end of the first few weeks of captivity, Ludwig and I had finished interpreting the barometer readings and other data obtained during our expedition, and writing a full account kept me busy until the end of December 1939. Of our British friends, we heard little. Johnny had not been allowed to leave India; as an RAF reservist, he had been called up at once. He had stored our equipment – tents, sleeping-bags, ropes and axes – in a school in Lahore. They not only survived the war, but eventually found their way back to the Vienna office of the Union of Students, who had lent them to us. Johnny wrote once or twice from Baluchistan, where he was stationed, then we heard no more.

Frank and Don got back safely to England, where my wife lived throughout the war, not as an internee, but working on the land. Frank kept in touch with her and saw to her welfare. He had also taken charge of our photographic films and my wife helped him to develop them. Officially he was not allowed to send us any prints, but one tiny, treasured picture did find its way to the camp: Ludwig's splendid photo of Mulkila taken from M1, the mountain we nicknamed Snowdrop. Each year on September 7, we celebrated the anniversary of climbing Mulkila with an extra orange and, until it became scarce, a piece of chocolate.

We attempted to learn Hindustani and other languages. Time passed quickly, but the war went on. The sky was our calendar. For nine months in the year it was cloudless. The moon waxed and waned. At first, we counted the full-moons; later, we counted the years. When Orion rose in the eastern sky, we knew that another year of captivity was behind us. Ahmednagar lies on the high plateau of the Deccan, where the stony half-desert stretches, flat as a table and almost treeless, as far as the eye can see. There was one solitary hill. When we looked beyond the tents and barracks towards the open spaces, our eyes were caught and held by the double-apron fence, for the fence was higher than all else in the surrounding plain. Barbed wire was our horizon. Once, after evening roll-call as the sun was setting, we thought we saw the distant gleam of snow, but it was the white-washed gable of a house. The illusion was almost perfect.

After some time, we and our guards were moved from Ahmednagar to Deolali and from there to Dehra Dun, at the foot of the Himalayas. But barbed wire is everywhere the same. At Dehra Dun the Camp Commandant took trouble to instil some variety into our existence. Study, sport and hobbies were encouraged, and he even allowed excursions on parole within the limits which the strict regulations allowed. In all those years, Ludwig and I never missed one outing. The prisoners were marched out of the camp in a body and were then allowed to split into groups. We usually asked a third to join us, a younger man named Fred. The three of us could afford to go some distance, as we were all tough and all able and willing to run the whole way back to camp.

In course of time, we were able to increase the radius of our excursions. For years we were allowed only half a day, then in Dehra Dun the time was increased to nine hours, the interval between morning and evening roll-call. By the strictest behaviour and discipline, we eventually persuaded our escorting guards to trust us completely, and they then used to settle themselves under a tree near the camp and sleep until we returned. Of the nine hours' freedom, one hour had to be deducted for the escorted march from the camp and back. We wondered if we could reach Mussoorie in the eight hours that remained, for it was the lights of that mountain spa which gleamed down to us at night from the ridge. From there, the great mountains of Garhwal might be visible.

Mussoorie was fifteen miles away and 5,000 feet above the camp. A route was soon reconnoitred through the wild terrain and those with health and stamina managed to get there. But the mountains were not always visible and there was hardly time even to sit down. We had to avoid the best viewpoints in case we were seen by British summer visitors, for that would have meant the end of our outings, at any rate in that part of the country.

Only once did we taste real joy. It was at Christmas time and we three had obtained permission to leave before morning roll-call to fetch a Christmas tree for the camp. How different it was, climbing in the clear morning air, compared with later, in the heat of the day! We spent a whole hour at Mussoorie, sitting in the sunshine and drinking in the splendour of the mountains. We identified Bandarpunch, which means the Monkey's Tail (20,720 feet), Chaukhamba, and the noble Nanda Devi (25,645 feet).

It was very late when we started to return. We had picked the Christmas tree on the way up, naturally from those nearest to the camp, as the whole affair was really a pretext. But we also wanted to be honest about it and we meant to go to real trouble to give our fellow prisoners a treat on Christmas Eve. The tree we chose was 13 feet high. With two of us carrying it down a steep winding path with stones underfoot, we soon discovered it was impossible to keep up a steady jog-trot, so we carried it in turn, one man at a time. When the first man had had enough of the ponderous thing, the second took over without interrupting the trot. In this way we managed to reach camp, true to our promise, in time for evening roll-call.

In 1942, Ludwig and I were summoned abruptly to the camp office. Following us with pistol at the ready, the guard reported: "Numbers 717 and 718 present, sir!" The officer smiled and led us to a room where a young, shining-eyed second lieutenant was sitting: Don Comber on his way to Burma. He brought us some small presents and, to our great delight, several minute photographs from our great expedition. We never saw him again, for Don was killed fighting in Burma.

About this time, the danger arose that the Japanese might overrun India. In that event, Ludwig and I had agreed to try to escape into the mountains. Ludwig's climbing boots had been new in 1939 and were still in good condition. My own, on the other hand, looked pathetic. Leather was becoming scarce even before I had left Vienna, and the best I could contrive was to have an old pair of boots re-soled. My father had given me another discarded pair of his own. After our climbs in Lahul both pairs were falling to pieces. In the prevailing uncertainty, I decided in 1942 to put at least one pair in good order with the remaining nails from both. Each day, after the potato-peeling fatigue was over, I cautiously withdrew one or two damaged clinker nails from the boots, taking great care not to break any. When they were all out, I hammered them straight as gently as though they were gold. The strongest nails were for the heels, the toes and the edges of the soles half-way along the boots. The most worn, those which had lost their wings, were for the middle of the soles. My father's boots were then re-soled by the camp cobbler and then the trickiest part of the work began – driving in the spikes, bending and hammering them so that the tips dug into the leather on the outer edge of the sole under the wings of the clinker, and finally clinching the nails. So as not to lose patience and ruin everything, I finished no more than two or three nails a day.

The Japanese did not appear, but the boots came into their own in 1944. In that year, Ludwig and I were released from captivity to take up teaching appointments in India, and that meant, of course, that we could not only dream of further expeditions to the Himalayas, but plan them.

CHAPTER 2

Solo

SPRING, 1945. The end of the war was in sight and it was about a year since I had been released from the internment camp. I had applied to be repatriated to Austria immediately hostilities ceased and, thinking my request would be granted, I now made up my mind to take a last look at the Himalayas.

The school where I worked was on a three weeks' holiday, but Ludwig would not be free till later, so I would have to go alone and, with little time and still less money, be content to gaze at the mountains. The rail journey alone, there and back, would take up nine of the twenty-one days, so, as in 1939, the train would have to take me to within striking distance of my objective. I chose the Nanda Devi Group. I had to get police permission to go further than five miles from my place of work, and as I aimed to travel over 1,200 miles, I applied for a permit some months beforehand and was duly granted one.

I got into the train at the southern tip of India at the beginning of May, and less than five days later reached the foot of the Garhwal Himalayas. There I took the bus from Kathgodam to Naini Tal, where I presented my permit to the senior police officer to whom it was addressed, and explained my plans to him. He kept the permit and told me to go ahead.

Naini Tal is a popular summer resort and boasts a small lake, a rarity in the Himalayas. Though the lakes in the Austrian and Swiss Alps are incomparably more beautiful, the cool waters at Naini Tal were wonderfully refreshing after the long, hot train journey. I hired a boat, rowed out to the middle of the lake, dived in and swam to my heart's content.

I spent the night in the YMCA hostel, finding it crowded with British troops. During supper, we heard Winston Churchill's speech announcing the end of the war in Europe. It was May 8, 1945.

On reaching Almora I went to the *dak* bungalow, though the high prices did not exactly suit my slender purse. But the registers of guests at these official rest-houses were very carefully kept in wartime and, by staying in one, I made it easier for the police to keep track of me. Judging from the lengthy correspondence I had had with them over my trip, I knew they would try and I thought it far better for them to succeed.

I wrote to my wife at this time: "The weight which prison life has left on my mind is lifting only slowly. Soon after my release, I thought I had already got over the past. But I was wrong." In fact there was not much difference between my life as an internee and as a teacher in southern India, except that I was now living among normal people instead of with eccentrics warped by long years of captivity. My movements were still restricted. I was still under surveillance – by the police now in place of the army. Of my personal belongings which had been confiscated in 1939, only three items remained when I was released from the internment camp: a camera, a compass and a sewing needle. The camera and compass were now with the police in Madura. The needle had been returned.

After studying maps of the area at a school in Almora, I decided on a walk to the Sarju Valley. On the fourth day the route would divide, the left fork leading to the Pindari Glacier and the right to the Kungribini Pass on the frontier of Tibet. I should have liked to see that frontier; I might even have climbed one of the mountains overlooking the pass and so caught a glimpse of Tibet, but for an ex-enemy alien to be seen in that area might cause trouble, and I made up my mind to content myself with hiking to the Pindari Glacier and enjoying the scenery on the way. The route is one of the oldest in the Himalayas and superbly beautiful; it is signposted and impossible to miss, so for that part of the tour I only needed to make a note of the distances between rest-houses. For the Kungribini Pass I made a pencil copy of the map.

As I only had eleven days, I took little food with me. Even so, the two-man tent and my climbing boots, which I decided to carry rather than wear, were a sore weight, and I had to look for a porter, after some difficulty hiring a mere boy who was too young to carry even half my load.

Almora is in a wonderful position, sited, like many villages in

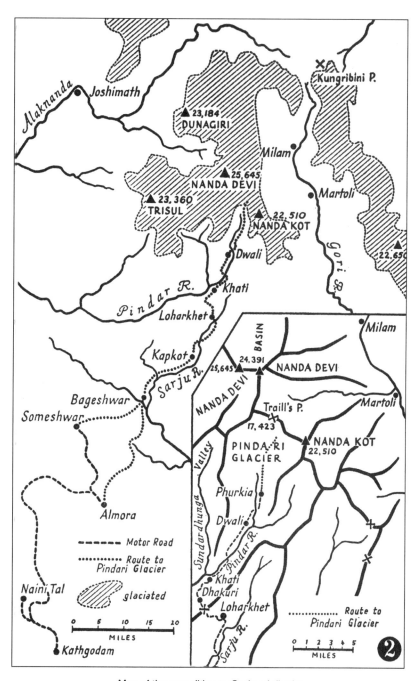

Map of the expedition to Garhwal district

northern India, on a crest of the Himalayan foothills so as to catch the cooler air. Below me to the south the Ganges plain shimmered in the summer heat, while to northward reared the icy peaks of some of the highest mountains in the world – Kamet, Trisul, Nanda Devi and Panchchuli. At that time of year, in May, walking from Almora towards the eternal snows was a wonderful experience. Well-tended tracks led along the ridges. There were walnut trees, cherry trees and apricots, and firs with giant cones; in many places the path was flanked by miniature pomegranate trees with bright red blossom. Everywhere one could hear the sad, insinuating tones of the silvered flute which every shepherd boy possesses.

Soon, alas, I had to go down into the valley, where the sparse firs gave no protection from the sun and the heat was like a furnace. My boy-porter lagged continually behind, and so held me up that I could afford only a short rest at midday if I was to keep up to schedule. Normally in India, men and animals crawl into the shade between noon and three o'clock, and I found it exhausting work carrying a heavy rucksack uphill and down over stony tracks in the heat of the day.

I reached Bageshwar, a sizeable place in the Sarju Valley, at the end of the second day's march, and to save money I slept in my tent instead of the rest-house. But first I had to find a better porter. I went to a tea-shop and as I was drinking a bowl of tea – served strong, the colour of cocoa, with milk and sugar already in it – a crowd of gapers collected outside. Unlike other Europeans, I was not wearing khaki shorts and a sun helmet, but a pair of dilapidated Tyrolean climbing breeches of light grey cloth and my good old Ortler hat. I knew this unusual garb would attract attention, but I preferred that to being accused of trying to escape by passing myself off as British. Speaking through the door – in their own language, not in English! – I asked the bystanders about porters. In 1939 I had known only a few words of Hindustani, but since then I had learnt a lot, and learnt it the hard way, from books, as an internee. It was impossible to practise conversation as the only Indians who came into the camps were the sweepers, and they spoke Mahratti, and the language in southern India where I worked after my release was Dravidian Tamil. Here, at last, in Bageshwar, was the first opportunity I had had to speak Hindustani and hear it spoken with the correct pronunciation of those difficult sounds we had tried in vain to puzzle out in the internment camp.

Eventually I found an oldish, down-at-heel fellow who undertook to carry my rucksack until I found somewhere to pitch the tent, and to be ready again next day at 6 a.m. We set off accompanied by a crowd of ragged Indians, all wearing the revolutionary headgear, the "Gandhi cap", as it was then called. I set up the tent by the river above the village and then – a moment I had been looking forward to all day – plunged into the cooling waters. Fifty yards away, the motley throng now seemed to be in earnest discussion. It was long after nightfall when they finally dispersed.

The next day's hike was long, dull and hot. My new porter was no better at keeping up, but at least he did not complain. I reached Kapkot in the afternoon and waited for him, intending to spend the night there. The place was full of troops on leave: British and American soldiers who had come to see the Himalayas, and Gurkhas who were on their way to their homes in the mountain villages. Following their example, I settled myself on the grass in front of the rest-house. It was too hot to spend the night in the house or under canvas. Nearby was a group of two British and three American soldiers. A young Englishman complained that he had not seen his wife for six months. I told him I sympathized. I had not seen mine for six years.

"Where is your wife?" he asked. "In Austria?"

"No. She is in England, in the Midlands."

"Did you say the Midlands?" interposed an American. "Whereabouts?"

"At a place called Cookley, near Kidderminster."

"We-ll! Can you beat that!" cried the American. "My wife's in Kidderminster right now. She works in the hospital. And I was stationed there. I know Cookley – know it from end to end!" But while we said what a small world it was, Fortune was turning her wheel. It was just getting dark when my porter suddenly came running up. With him was a squad of Indian police. "There is the man!" said the porter and three panting, perspiring policemen arrested me on the spot. This made everyone sit up. What offence was I supposed to have committed? "Escaping," said the police. I told them that I had not escaped from anywhere, that I was on a pleasure trip for which I had obtained official approval and that I had been given a permit. The men refused to believe me. They were deaf, too, to the arguments of the British and American soldiers, who, after the details I had given them about my wife in England, felt they could swear to my *bona fides*. Very interesting, said the police. But they had their orders, and their orders said: back to Bageshwar! So now, into the rest-house with you, German!

That was too much. Suddenly my patience snapped and I told the police that I refused to go into the rest-house and if they tried to force me, I should resist. "Quite right, too!" joined in the soldiers – and there were a lot of them. So the police gave way and squatted round me where I lay on the grass. But it was a long time before I could sleep. The earth was warm still and the air sultry. In the forest beyond the nearby river, the brain-fever bird was calling, repeating its plaintive cadence at regular intervals. What did the fellows want with me? I turned from side to side, but could find no answer. Of course I had not escaped, but perhaps that was not what they wanted me for. Perhaps I was going to be repatriated. That was it. I felt sure it was. I had applied to be sent home as soon as the war was over, and it was over – just. No. Official machinery could never move as fast as that. It was too soon to expect repatriation. Well, then, what did the fellows want with me? Again, I tried to analyse the situation. What had I done to deserve this? Nothing. Then why were they arresting me? It was just a stupid mistake. Could I clear it up in Bageshwar or would I have to go all the way back to Almora? And how much holiday would be left by the time I got there? But surely they could not believe I had escaped – where from? From an internment camp? But I had been released!

My thoughts went round and round; I just could not stop them, until finally I had to force them away from the subject by trying to fit the call of the brain-fever bird (what a good name!) into a musical notation. It was not easy, and somewhere in an interval between calls I must have fallen asleep.

The march back to Bageshwar started early next morning. The police engaged porters to carry the luggage.

"But where is my own porter?" I asked.

"Gone home," said one of the policemen.

"But I have not paid him yet!"

The man smiled. "*Pagal hai*" was the reply, which meant: "We know him; he's crazy."

As we walked the three men questioned me, trying to make me contradict myself. Obviously, they did not believe one word of my story. I had escaped, hadn't I, from an internment camp? Come now! They looked rather aggrieved when I persisted in saying "No." Finally, they gave up, apparently with no hard feelings but just the reverse – with something like admiration for this man who could tell such bare-faced lies with such obstinate conviction.

On our way, we met some local inhabitants coming up the valley. They asked the policemen who I was and were told: "An escaped prisoner, a German."

"Then let him go!" they shouted.

The policemen shook their heads and tried to move on. Then the people turned on the porters. "You miserable rascals! Put that stuff down!" Finally, one of them shouted at the police: "You ought to be ashamed of yourselves, arresting this man! He has escaped from the British, hasn't he?"

The campaign for Indian independence was then at its height and the best that British people could expect was a cold reception. But as soon as the natives discovered I was German – few had even heard of Austria – they were friendly and helpful. When I left India three years later, the situation was completely different. Germany had ceased to exist as far as Indians were concerned, but, having achieved their independence, they were prepared to tolerate those Britons who had remained in the country.

Towards noon, my guards decided to have tea. The tea-shops on this pilgrim's route consist of mud huts. The floor is always clean, a layer of diluted cow-dung being spread over it to keep down the dust. Straw mats are provided to sit on. There is also usually a chárpái – that is, a wooden bedstead with a covering of plaited straw or coconut matting. The only source of light is the doorway. The tea is made as an infusion. Small linen bags containing the tea leaves are put in boiling water which has been heated in a kettle over a primitive hearth of two stones, or simply a niche in the mud wall. The tea is served scalding hot, with milk and sugar already added, in a brass bowl standing in a large, deep saucer. The saucer is taken in the left hand and the bowl in the right, and the tea is poured from one to the other until it is cool enough to drink. You start with the bowl and saucer rim to rim and, still pouring, gradually draw them further apart until they are at arm's length. As the right arm rises with the bowl, a long jet of tea seems to be drawn out of the saucer.

The man who served us was curious to know who I was and the policemen repeated the story I had already heard so often, I presumed it was included in their written orders. They said I was an escaped German internee disguised as a *sadhu* – that is, a Hindu who has dedicated his life to God. I doubt whether they had seen a *sadhu* disguised as a Tyrolese before, but that did not seem to worry them. The policemen brought me some tea, drank several basinfuls themselves and then prepared to sleep until four. I protested in vain that I wanted to get to Bageshwar as soon as possible so that my wrongful arrest could be cleared up. "If we march at this time of day we will get heat-stroke," they said. They were right, of course, so I had to submit. We ate *chapátis* and then put our heads down. But I could not sleep, and after a while I asked if I could bathe in the nearby river. After much hesitation, this was allowed. I bathed until three, then returned to the hut, hoping we would leave. But the senior policeman, a very energetic and, I should think, very efficient man of about thirty-five, said politely but firmly: "Sahib, it is still too early. The sun is too high. It would burn pitilessly on the back of our necks. Have patience, O Sahib, and I will help to pass the time. I will sing you a song about a hero, an Indian hero who was greater than Hitler. Stronger and more daring than Hitler."

The other two policemen and the owner of the tea-shop squatted expectantly with their backs to the mud wall and with a sigh of resignation I sat down on the bed. Then the man began to sing, softly at first, sustaining certain syllables with a kind of trill. I could see that he was completely carried away by the story he told. It was in verse and he improvised the tune, suiting it to the matter, somewhat as children do, when instead of telling some tale or other in a normal voice they chant it. Sometimes he sang *fortissimo* and in the confined space his voice swelled to a thunder. Then he would stop dramatically and, turning to me, say quietly: "You see, Sahib, what a strong man he was?"

At first I felt too impatient to follow the story; then the singer's enthusiasm and the others' rapt attention laid their spell on me and I began to listen. The story was difficult to follow as I had

never read any Hindi verse or heard it declaimed, but I understood enough to recognize the Epic of Rama:

Ayodhya, the royal city, has no equal upon Earth.
It is impregnable. The main street is forever strewn
With flowers and young maidens disport themselves.
Gardens and mango orchards abound. Rice is never lacking.
For water the people drink the sweet sap of the sugar cane.
In their gladness the people make sweet music to sound
From dawn until dusk: fanfares, trumpets, lutes and drums.

Now there ruled formerly in Ayodhya a mighty Prince
And hosts of lesser princes were subject to him.
But King Dasharatha had one great sorrow:
He lacked a son to whom he might bequeath his kingdom.
Then the wise men counselled him to make a sacrifice
And, in truth, three of his wives bore sons.
The first wife bore Rama, and the second, Bharata,
And the third wife bore the twins, Lakshmana and Shatrughna.

All four sons grew to be mighty heroes, for in them
The God Vishnu had become man in order to slay the Rakshasa,
The Evil Demons whom the God Brahma in his guilelessness
Had so made at the time of the Creation that neither gods,
Demi-gods nor animals could overcome them, but only men.
Against these the Demons demanded no protection,
Considering them to be powerless and contemptible creatures.

Rama was fifteen years of age when, with the help
Of miraculous weapons, he killed the she-demon, Tankata
Who was strong with the strength of a thousand elephants.
Now at the court of the King of Mithila there lived
The fairest of all maidens, Sita. Sita was born of the Earth.
The King had reared her as his own daughter and promised her
As wife to the man who could bend the mighty bow of Vishnu
Which lay in the King's armoury. Many had tried to bend it,
But none had succeeded. When Rama came to win Sita
Fifty hundreds of strong men drew out the bow
In an eight-wheeled cart. Rama bent it with ease.
Rama led the fair and submissive Sita to Ayodhya.

The time came at last when the King of Ayodhya
Felt his end approaching. Then he chose Rama,
His eldest son, whom the people loved for
His modesty and wisdom, to rule with him.
Already the city was being decked with garlands
And banners for the crowning, when the hunch-backed
Favourite of Kaikeyi, the mother of Bharata,
Came running to her mistress and conjured her
To demand banishment for Rama and the throne
For her own son. Then Kaikeyi sent one of her women
To the King. "O King!" she cried. "Come! The wife
Whom thou most lovest lies low and weeps."

The King found Kaikeyi lying naked on the bare earth,
Sobbing bitterly. So the hunch-backed woman had advised,
Knowing her mistress' allurements. The King knelt down,
Felt the dark hair of his wife and pleaded:
"Tell me, O Kaikeyi, of thy great sorrow!
Whatever thy desire, I will grant it."
Then, half raising herself, Kaikeyi gazed to heaven
Through the water that filled her black eyes
And cried: "Ye three-and-thirty gods! Ye have heard
His promise! This, O King, is my desire.
Thou shalt Make Bharata to rule with thee and Rama thou shalt banish
For fourteen years into the wilderness."

Then the old king thought his heart would break.
Defenceless before a woman's wiles, he was caught
With his own promise. "As thou spakest, so it shall be."
When Rama heard of this his face darkened with rage.
Lakshmana urged him to take up arms. But Rama thought
Of his old father writhing in the toils of conflicting duties.
What if right were on Rama's side when only submission Could bring his
    father peace? So he laid aside his
Princely garments and took up the wanderer's staff.

Loudly lamenting, the people went with Rama to the city gate.
The sacred fires would not kindle; the sun hid her face;
The planets fell smoking from their spheres.
Rama, Lakshmana and Sita wandered far to the south.
By a beautiful mountain they built a hut and there lived
In poverty and prayer. Years passed, then tidings came
How the demons waxed insolent, working mischief
Throughout the land. In the middle of the forest
In the demons' abode, Rama built a new hut and from there
Gave battle while a vulture watched over Sita.
Fourteen thousand evil-doers he slayed with arrows
Given him by the God Brahma. When he heard of this
At Lanka on the island of Ceylon, the Demon King
By cunning led Sita away captive and wounded the vulture.

The vulture flew to Rama and Rama ranged through the forest,
Desperate and loudly lamenting, but Sita he could not find.
But the golden haired King of the Apes, Sugriva,
Promised Rama his help. He sent out his apes to find Sita
And at Lanka in Ceylon the King's Minister, the
Ape, Hanumat, found her. Then Sugriva called together
His army and sent it with Hanumat and Rama to Ceylon.
Lanka was destroyed and the Demon King fell and was killed
By Rama in single combat. Sita, released, wept for joy.

But doubt gnawed at Rama's heart. Surely Sita had smiled
Upon the Demon King? Then Sita told Rama how the King
Had spoken to her. "Thou, Sita, art the fairest among women.
No man can resist thee. Thy limbs are like the trunks
Of elephants. Thy hips are broad, thy waist is as a twig

For slimness. But hear, I beseech thee! I will not use
Force upon thee: give me thy love!" So spake the Demon.
But Sita spurned him. To Rama she swore her innocence.
But Rama believed her not. Then, full of shame, the fair Sita
Ascended the funeral pyre. But see! The flames spared her
And Rama saw and repented him. Joyfully with his bride
He set his feet towards Ayodhya and home.
The story of Rama and his wondrous deeds sped before him
And came to his brother Bharata who ruled in his father's stead.
Much time had passed and the old king had died.
But Rama had not been forgotten and in all the city
The people sang of his virtue. Would Bharata hear them?
Bharata was not proud and sought to emulate his brother
In well-doing. He greeted the hero and bowed down to him
As the rightful and lawful king. So Rama ruled over Ayodhya.
And Rama ruled for ten times a thousand and ten times
One hundred years. And poverty and hunger were no more.
Sickness was forgotten. There were no more widows, no more
Parents bereft of their children. Wives were faithful
Unto their husbands. Fire became the servant of man.
Storm and flood were tamed and the people were happy
Under Rama, the hero, their King.

This was the story that the young man sang. When he had finished he smiled and got up. My escort made ready and we stepped from the semi-darkness of the tea-shop into the brilliance of the afternoon sun.

The Epic of Rama was written over 2,000 years ago by the Indian poet, Valmiki. It was written in Sanskrit, and comprised 24,000 verses. My Indian guard knew by heart a few hundred verses of a popular Hindi translation. It is said that the early singers told the story so graphically that people believed it was a matter of recent history. With his repeated reference to Hitler, the policeman showed that he, too, perhaps, believed that the battle between the demi-god Rama and the Demon King had only just come to an end.

Tired and thirsty, we reached Bageshwar that same evening. I had given up hope of finding anyone there who could order my release and, as there was no telephone, knew that I would have to wait until Almora. The police locked me up for the night in a small room about the size of a lavatory. They apologized that nothing better was available and brought what they could to add to my comfort: a bowl of water to wash in, a pillow and tea and *chapátis* with vegetables. A good dozen individuals came and gazed at me in my hutch, including some of the shabby youths who had stood chattering by my tent two days before. So they were informers! How much, I wondered, had they been paid for putting the police on the wrong trail?

I spent an uncomfortable night, and next morning a further trial awaited me. Two of the men were to take me over the mountains to Almora; the third, the singer of the previous day, gave me a firm handshake and bade me a dignified farewell. Then, before we set off I was told that we would have to be inoculated! For myself I flatly refused, but I still had to wait for over an hour until the doctor appeared for the two policemen. At last we set off northwards and marched through narrow, sparsely wooded valleys in broiling heat, going a different way than I had come and heading for the village of Baijnath, where a bus could take us on the last stage of the journey to Almora.

Just before we reached the top of a pass we had a curious encounter. Coming down towards us where we were resting by a spring we saw a well equipped party with several mules, drivers, and, bringing up the rear, two white men and two good-looking women in mountaineering costume. In the course of conversation, I discovered that they were British officers doing service in India and were intending to explore the Sundardhunga area, on the fringe of the Nanda Devi Basin. How I envied them and, by contrast, felt the full wretchedness of my own luck! The leader of the party had climbed in Austria and remembered it with evident pleasure. When I told him of my arrest he tried to console me, saying that as the police already knew of my walking tour, the reason could only be my early repatriation. I hoped he was right, but it seemed too improbable.

Just as Swiss Alpine guides use the same spot on their mountains for their breakfast-halt, so my escort had a definite tea-shop in mind for the midday siesta. Owing to our late start, we did not reach it until three and by then it was shut. We sat down in the shade of the building and one of the policemen made a meal for the three of us. It was quickly done. He took some black, coarsely ground flour from a small bag, kneaded it into a dough with salt and water, then beat it between the palms of his hands into a thin disc. The disc was put into an iron pan and cooked over a fire which the other man had made – and the meal was ready. Day in, day out, these *chapátis* are the staple diet in northern India, as rice is in the south.

"Forgive us, Sahib, that we have no butter!" said the cook. "Otherwise we would look for certain plants in the field here and fry them as vegetables. But policemen are not well paid. Forgive us, Sahib!"

We reached Baijnath towards evening, only to find that the bus had gone. For me, that meant another night in the lock-up. Next day, as though to make amends, my guards gave me precedence in the Battle for the Bus. It was already full to the roof when we got to it and I had to climb in through a window. How the two policemen managed to get on board I never knew, as I only saw them when we reached Almora. Probably, they rode on the mudguards.

It was evening when at long last we entered the Superintendent's office in Almora. My two escorts had polished themselves up. I, on the other hand, had had no such opportunity and must have looked as though I had escaped from a dustbin. The Superintendent of Police eyed me with a somewhat supercilious smile on his face and then said, more as a statement of fact than a question:

"So you escaped from the internment camp in Dehra Dun?"

I was not in a good humour and saw no reason to conceal the fact. "I have not escaped from anywhere," I said. "You have made a most foolish mistake. I am on a walking tour – or was. I am on holiday from the school where I work in southern India. The authorities there have known about this trip for the last four months, and ought to have informed you up here."

The Superintendent had clearly not expected this and felt that the safest course was to "pass the baby" to his superior, the District Commissioner, to whom I was duly presented and repeated my story. When I had finished there was a pause. It was really laughable, but he did not believe me, either.

"All you have to do," I said, "is to lift the telephone and speak to the Police Station at Naini Tal. They took my permit; they told me it was in order. They will tell you that every word I have said is true."

So the Commissioner lifted the telephone, and my story was confirmed. But there was one last point. On arrival at Almora, had I signed the register at the *dak* bungalow with my real name? Again the Commissioner lifted the telephone, this time to speak to the *chawkidar* of the rest-house, and was told that I had. So there was nothing for it – the Commissioner had to apologize and set me free.

But now that the nightmare was over I felt in no mood to rejoice. My most carefully planned holiday had been ruined. I had spent a lot of money for nothing and in exactly six days I would have to start the return journey to southern India. Had I time to walk to the Pindari Glacier? It was supposed to take eight days from Almora. Five days was considered the minimum. I decided I would try to do it in three.

There was no point, of course, in engaging a porter. At the speed I planned to keep up, I should have to carry my own rucksack. As for food, I would take an iron ration of dried fruit and for the rest would rely on getting tea and *chapátis* at the villages *en route*. I would wear gym shoes, so as to move faster, and take neither ice-axe nor climbing boots. These could stay behind in Almora. And if there seemed any risk of getting blisters, I would go barefoot.

On the first day I walked over forty miles, from Almora to Kapkot, where I had been arrested. Somehow, the villagers had already heard of my release and they welcomed me as a friend. Even the policeman was a changed man and entertained me to a meal of *chapátis* with wild vegetables fried in butter. It seemed the villagers had only just heard of the end of the war in Europe.

"*Germany har gaya. Sach hai?*" asked the policeman. "Is it true that Germany has been defeated?"

"*Sach hai,*" I replied. "It is true."

Just beyond Kapkot came that tempting fork in the road that I had noted when planning my holiday. The left-hand route was the one usually taken by tourists wanting to see a Himalayan glacier at close quarters. If I kept to the right, I would eventually reach the Kungribini Pass and the Tibetan frontier. Tibet … But it was no use. From the very start I had decided it would be better not to be seen wandering in the frontier zone. Now, after my interlude with the police, it would be doubly foolish. Besides, even if I had had the time, I had given my word to the police in Almora not to go that way. So, regretfully, I turned left.

At first the path led up a narrow valley flanked by steep mountain slopes. Far below, to the east there were glimpses of the river Sarju winding through a gorge, while a mile or two to the west the Pindari flowed parallel to the route from its source in the Pindari Glacier. To reach the glacier I had to cross a high, intervening ridge. The last rest-house on the near side of the pass was at Loharkhet, which in English means Smith's Field. Loharkhet lies high above the valley on a mountain slope, and, after a short midday rest there enjoying the splendid views, I climbed up to the pass. The weather had been fine all morning, but now I found myself shut in by grey clouds. Only a bird singing somewhere out of sight helped to relieve the gloom. It began to rain even before I reached the watershed and I could see there was a storm coming up. The only way in which I could keep up to my schedule was to run whenever I came to a down-slope and on the far side of the pass I did so – luckily, for I was in the doorway of the next rest-house when the storm broke and the sky turned to a cataract.

I found some British soldiers on leave in the rest-house and though I had gone for a couple of days without food in the mountains at home I was very grateful for their gift of some unwanted iron rations. Later in the afternoon, as I was going down towards Khati in the Pindari Valley, the weather cleared and, as it seemed to be set fine, I decided to press on to Dwali, so beating all records by covering the distance between four rest-houses in one day. But it took my last ounce of energy. For a mile beyond Khati the route kept close to the river, and here the scenery was among the wildest and most beautiful I have encountered in the Himalayas. On either side of the river, huge cliffs towered up into the darkening sky and the whole ravine echoed with the sound of the roaring waters. In several places, where rocks barred further progress, wooden bridges had to be crossed. Wherever the clefts were large enough, tall, slim firs and pines had taken root in the granite walls, their tops filtering what feeble light remained in the narrow strip of sky above the ravine.

It was almost dark by the time I reached the rest-house at Dwali. The old man in charge lit a fire for me in the open hearth, and what a joy it was! I took a foot-bath and then, tired as I was, forced myself to massage my aching leg muscles in preparation for the next day's climb up to the Pindari Glacier. The caretaker was a man of few words, but he knew how to look after his visitors. He made me a simple meal and with the last mouthful I fell like a sack on to the bed, waking next morning only when the birds told me that dawn was near and it was time to be on my way.

I had been the only traveller at Dwali. The next and last resthouse on the way to the glacier was at Phurkia. I reached it early that same morning, just as a party of British and American soldiers were leaving the hut to return to Almora. This was a stroke of luck, as there was no one in charge of the place and they had left a fire burning in the hearth where, having eaten nothing that day, I could quickly make some soup.

I had already crossed patches of frozen snow between Dwali and Phurkia, but here, near the rest-house, the slopes were covered with it. Being without climbing boots or ice-axe, I would have waited for the sun to soften the snow if I could have spared the time. As it was, I had to do my best in gym shoes with a rough, improvised walking-stick. The shoes, incidentally, were a size too large and to use them at all I had to wear two pairs of socks. Their soles had worn completely smooth. Thus equipped I had to cross a wide expanse of rock-hard snow on a slope which in places shot steeply down to the river roaring some hundreds of feet below.

I confess I thought of turning back. The soldiers had left tracks from the previous day, but they were too shallow for my slippery soles. Nothing less than steps freshly cut by an expert would have been of much help. So I worked my way diagonally up the slope, using what footholds I could find: avalanche debris, the sharp edges of channels cut by ice that had melted and then frozen again, odd pieces of rock scattered over the snow. And then, wherever I could see a spot below me where a rock, a dwarf fir or the natural contours of the slope gave a guarantee that I could stop myself, I went running and sliding down in a straight line. Never, in thirty years of mountaineering had I tried glissading in such conditions before, and though I could tell from experience how much grip I could expect from the different surfaces, though the discipline previously acquired on lone climbs enabled me that morning to take not one incautious step in many thousands that were certainly risky, and though I was not hampered by fear, I was indeed plagued by doubts of the sanity of risking my life in this way. Whenever I got stuck temporarily and could see nothing below to act as a stop, or above to climb up by, this thought – that I was not so much braving death as gambling with it – returned to my mind.

But ultimately the slopes flattened out, the glacier came into view, the sun softened the snow and I could use some of the existing tracks. Hurrying on to make up for lost time, I came to a lateral moraine and scrambling along it, reached the end of my journey at a point where the moraine abutted on to a smooth wall of rock. The distance from Almora was painted up in red letters, but I have forgotten it. The height above sea-level was 12,500 feet.

From where I was standing, the huge Pindari Glacier bursting forth in the centre of the picture looked impressive but not beautiful, and the surrounding mountains were too close to be seen in perspective. The source of the glacier and, on that particular day, Nanda Devi itself were invisible. If I made that pilgrimage a second time, it would not be for the view of the glacier, but for the sake of the journey itself and for the wonderful views of Trisul, Nanda Devi and Nanda Kot which, assuming better weather than I had, can be enjoyed on the way.

I took a long rest on a snow-free patch of rock in the moraine. The journey from Almora had taken me two and a half days, so that I had three days for the return trek and could take things a little more easily. Thus my first stage, that same afternoon, only took me a distance of twenty miles, as far as Khati. There I met the members of the British Sundardhunga expedition. It appeared that I had passed them unawares on the previous day while they were shopping in the village. They told me they were leaving the beaten track next day for the Sundardhunga Valley. I heard later that on their return they were in that same rest-house at Khati when a severe earthquake occurred. The chimney came crashing down into the kitchen, but luckily no one was hurt.

From the pass above Loharkhet, I climbed a grassy mountain of about 10,500 feet in the hope that a rift in the serried clouds would grant me a glimpse of Nanda Devi, the queen of the Central Himalayas. When I reached the summit there was no sign of a break; the air was warm and still, and there was absolutely nothing to be seen. But having got there, I felt it was a pity to leave straightaway and I waited for an hour. At the end of that time, when the clouds seemed as solid as ever, I was just starting the descent when suddenly, as if by magic, a rift appeared. Through it I could see an enormous ice-field glittering in the sun. I waited, hoping that the rift would widen. Then something made me look up and there, above the clouds, like some vision from another world, the magnificent icy peak of Nanda Kot was slowly appearing through the haze. For a few seconds only the apparition stayed, shining in immaculate splendour; then it was gone. But in my mind it will never fade.

Judging by this view of Nanda Kot and by a glimpse of the ice-field on Trisul which I had seen during the first part of my trip shimmering fifty miles away through the afternoon mist, I would say that the mountains in this area were more impressive than those of Lahul, not only because of their higher altitudes, but because the low-lying valleys enhanced their relative height. I had also seen and admired Nanda Devi from Almora, but at close range had glimpsed no more than the bold, upward sweeping lines of its mighty base.

The Garhwal Himalayas will always occupy an important place in the history of the highest mountains climbed. In 1907, for instance, Longstaff climbed Trisul (23,360 feet), until 1930 the highest summit ever attained. In 1931, Smythe conquered Kamet (25,447 feet). Then in 1936, Odell and Tilman reached the summit of Nanda Devi (25,645 feet), a record unbroken until Herzog and Lachenal climbed Annapurna in 1950.

My second journey to the Himalayas ended with an evening of utter peacefulness in the rest-house at Takula outside Almora. In the scented pine-woods the birds were singing with full-throated rapture. I was the only guest. While the Indian got my meal, I sat in a deck-chair in front of the rest-house and closed my eyes. Soon, pictures began to chase through my mind: of surging glacier streams, of a silver mountain towering above massed white clouds, of wheat growing in a golden band in some deep and tortuous valley, of a bird, brilliant in red, blue and green plumage, gliding with outstretched wings over a mountain gorge, of a rhododendron flower of delicate pale violet, and of brown, friendly Gurkha faces.

One by one, the birds fell asleep and darkness glowered from the trees. I thought of Austria. How I longed to see it again, even in chaos and misery.

CHAPTER 3

The Lost Mountain

WHILE I was on the way back to southern India from Almora, Ludwig Krenek was travelling north from Udaipur to pay a second visit to Lahul. Not only had he two months' holiday before him, but he had found a companion in Fabian Geduldig, who had been with us in internment. So Ludwig's second Himalayan journey was beginning more auspiciously than mine. But Fabian had only modest climbing experience in the Austrian Alps and could only stay away for three weeks. Moreover, right at the start Ludwig had a bad attack of malaria, a disease which he had originally contracted as an internee. So the two men had to rule out any thought of climbing mountains to the summit. All the same, they succeeded in adding considerably to the geographical knowledge of the area acquired in 1939 and Ludwig wrote the study on the glaciers of Lahul which we had planned before leaving Austria. He also discovered a pass near the Milang Basin which will be of practical use to future visitors, and before his holiday was over he explored an area near the Bara Shigri, twenty-five miles south-east of the Rohtang Pass, whose jagged peaks had so inspired me in 1939 that Johnny had marked them in our sketch-map: "Fritz's Favourites".

About the time of Ludwig's visit to Lahul, a second attempt to climb Mulkila was made by Italian prisoners-of-war from Dharmshala. A camp had been set up for them there in 1942. After Italy had made a separate peace with the Allies in the following year, the regulations were progressively relaxed and Italian officers were allowed to undertake trips into the mountains. By 1945 they were being granted leave of absence – on parole, of course – for weeks at a time. In the early summer of that year, two parties attacked Mulkila, one from the side we had

Ludwig Krenek, with the camera *(Fabian Geduldig);*
Fabian Geduldig *(Ludwig Krenek)*

chosen and the other from the north, the opposite side. Unfortunately, neither attempt succeeded.

Meanwhile, my hopes of early repatriation were beginning to fade. I did all I could to hasten it, but to no avail. When I found I could borrow the money, I offered to pay my fare; I even applied to work my passage, but it made not the slightest differences I was told I could not hope to find a berth inside a year, as not only British troops but British civilians were streaming home in anticipation of Indian independence and, understandably, all these people had priority over the one-time possessor of a German passport. As for working my passage, I never really expected to be taken on, there being doubtless many better qualifications for the post of steward in a big liner than a doctorate of philosophy. All the same, some Austrians had got home from England, though very few, and only those after careful quadripartite screening. I was only too eager to be screened, but even to be a candidate for the sieve required friends at Court, which, alas, I had not got.

Thus, soon after my return from Almora it became clear to me that I would still be in India for the winter holidays, which lasted from October until Christmas. In that case, I might be able to climb one of the big Himalayan mountains. Near Madura, where I worked, there was a Jesuit University which possessed excellent maps. After studying them I decided to attempt Gurla Mandhata (25,500 feet). As early as 1905 Dr. Longstaff had made a courageous effort to reach the summit and some decades later Dr. Tichy had tried again, but had been forced to turn back. I now wrote to Dr. Longstaff to find out what chance there was of success in the wintertime. The other problem was to find at least one other person to go with me. I knew Ludwig would not be able to get away from his school at that time of year, so I wrote to my British acquaintance whom I had met on the pass beyond Almora. He was later to be a member of the 1953 expedition that conquered Everest. He replied that he would have liked to come, but had no hope of getting leave. That was the first snag; the second, that it seemed impossible to predict if or when official permission could be obtained to travel to the tip of Tibet in which the mountain lay. So, by the time Dr. Longstaff's letter arrived, I had more or less given up the plan. But his straightforward, enthusiastic tone gave me great pleasure. "All good luck to you," he wrote, "and to dear Austria."

When it proved impossible to arrange a trip for the winter of 1945, I began to think of the following summer. I might still be in India and, if so, might arrange to be free. My contract with the school expired in May 1946, and I was not obliged to renew it or seek some other employment immediately. Ludwig would then be having his holidays. While continuing to send off applications for a travel permit to Gurla Mandhata, I now wrote to Ludwig suggesting we should do some climbing together in the summer of 1946, making it clear that I should have to leave him in the lurch if a chance of repatriation occurred. He, I knew, was in no hurry, but was thinking of staying in India. He replied from Udaipur: "Yes."

Still hoping that when the time came I should be on my way home, I started nevertheless to prepare in earnest for a trip to the Himalayas in the following year. On Sunday afternoons I dried vegetables in the hot sun. I picked an extremely acid-tasting fruit called *nellikai* from its thorny bushes and dried it as well, intending to inflict it on myself and my mountaineering companions for the sake of its vitamin C content. Some kind ladies darned the holes in my socks. I also went into training. The school was sited on a mountain that rises over 6,800 feet above the plains of southern India and on my days off I did training climbs, starting with the descent and ending with a climb up to the school again about midday. Readers who have never been in those latitudes can hardly conceive the difference between the hill climate and the oppressive heat in the plain. Travelling down from the school by bus felt like being plunged into a Turkish bath. I found it took some effort to climb up again out of that atmosphere.

I also climbed some rock faces, and the most rugged pinnacle in the massif succumbed to my second attempt. The main obstacles, actually, were cacti and bramble thickets, and, potentially, snakes, tigers, panthers, bison and elephants, or, at any rate, it seemed so to me, wandering alone in the jungle and unarmed except at times with an umbrella which I had used in Lahul before the war as a sunshade. Once, when making my way past a large herd of sheep and goats, I put it up suddenly to see what the effect would be. I was amazed: one look at the shining black saucer and the herd scattered in all directions. Would tigers have done the same?

Soon, sketch-maps and interesting suggestions began to arrive from Ludwig in Udaipur and, from time to time, a letter from official A about the permit for Gurla Mandhata advising me to apply to official B. My British acquaintance of the previous spring also wrote, inviting me to join an expedition to Nun, a 23,400-foot mountain in Kashmir, but I was now committed to a last fling with Ludwig.

I should have liked to attempt one of the Himalayan giants and one only, so as to try out all the ideas on the organization and technique of a big climb which I had thought out in the internment camps. But as there would be only two of us – our potential third, the man who helped with the Christmas tree in Dehra Dun, was still behind barbed wire – and as we could not afford to employ porters from Darjeeling, the choice was very restricted. Of the mountains over 26,000 feet, I could find none that would suit us. Some of the peaks near K2 and Mount Everest, which we might have considered, were ruled out simply because they were too far away. There were several 26,000-footers in Nepal, including some of the less difficult ones, but at that time Nepal was rigorously closed to outside visitors. There remained only Nanga Parbat and Kangchenjunga, but to attack either of these two giants with the means at our disposal would have been to emulate the folly of the man who tried climbing Everest alone and lost his life in the attempt. So I suggested either Gurla Mandhata or Rakaposhi near Gilgit in Kashmir, both of which are over 25,000 feet. Ludwig agreed on the assumption that we were going to attempt one big mountain, but pointed out that as we would not be able to afford porters, my plan would entail long marches to and fro over the same ground taking up supplies for the intermediate camps. Rather than do this, Ludwig wrote that he would prefer to explore some less well known group of mountains. This was sensible and I asked him to choose a suitable area in case my plan had to be cancelled for lack of a travel permit.

We both realized that if the venture did come off, it would have to be done very much on the cheap. I was earning very little and Ludwig, at his school in Udaipur, even less. Our only equipment consisted of remnants from 1939. For food, we would have to depend on rice and *chapátis*. We had too little of everything, in fact, except time, and really our funds were so ludicrously small that if it had not been for the knowledge we had acquired of how to get along cheaply in India, and for Ludwig's really excellent Hindustani, we would never have ventured into the Himalayas at all.

The total cost of a Himalayan expedition varies, of course, according to the objective and the area in which it lies, the numbers taking part and the manner in which they are organized. Comparisons which take none of this into account are therefore useless. But it is interesting to consider, in individual cases, the cost of the voyage to India, say, in relation to the other expenses of the expedition, for this will give some idea of the outlay in the actual climbing area. In our case, in 1939, the voyage cost £45 per head and the local expenses were also £45 per head. In many expedition reports it will be found that the latter were about ten times the cost of the journey by sea. The difference is chiefly accounted for by the number of porters employed. In 1939, we had twenty porters to carry our equipment up to the base camp; in 1946, twelve. On many expeditions some hundreds of porters are employed.

Of course, the number of porters required depends on the numbers in the expedition, the height of the peaks to be climbed and the length of the approach route, and our holiday trip was modest in all these respects. But economy can be exercised in attempts on even the highest mountains, as Tilman and Shipton proved in 1938 when they occupied Camp VI on Everest at a cost of £2,000, as compared with the £10,000 spent on each of the elaborate Everest expeditions between 1922 and 1938. Tilman and Shipton have broken many a lance in mountaineering literature in favour of less elaborate Himalayan expeditions, but strangely enough they have not had the support that might have been expected from German-speaking mountaineers.

*   *   *   *

Eleven months had passed since the end of the war and the question of my return to Austria was as obscure as ever. Meanwhile, I was doing all I could to end the separation from my wife. The British Government had no objection to Martha remaining in England, but refused me an entry permit so that I could join her. Similarly, the Indian Government did not mind me, but would not have her. So she from England and I from India wrote to some of the ex-neutral countries, begging their assistance. Only two replied – both in the negative. Finally, in despair, I wrote two letters, one to New Delhi and the other to London, asking whether some loophole might not be found in the regulations for the exercise of a little humanity and compassion, and, miraculously, an Indian official did find it, with the result that in April, 1946, shortly before my teacher's contract was due to expire, I was notified from New Delhi that Martha would be allowed to join me in India after the completion of certain formalities. How grateful we were – and still are! – to that anonymous civil servant!

But we felt we should only choose this solution if there was no alternative. For seven years Martha had ploughed fields, milked cows and kept farm accounts in England and her savings would cover the cost of her fare to India. But how should the two of us get from India to Austria? It would be impossible to borrow the price of a double fare, and to earn it in India would take years. If we were both in England, on the other hand, at least our repatriation to Austria – if it ever came – would not be held up for lack of

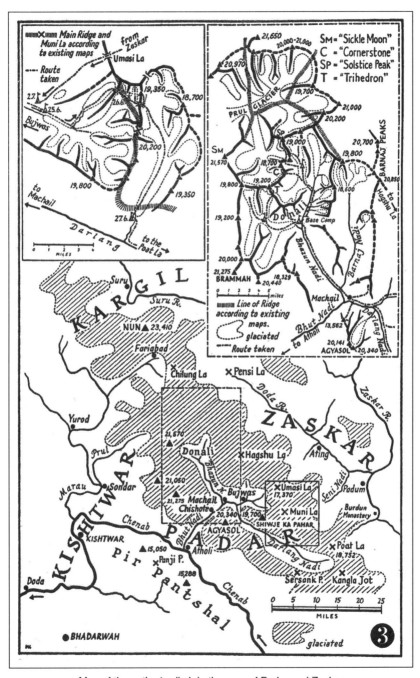

Map of the author's climb in the area of Padar and Zaskar

money on our part. Before accepting the Indian offer, therefore, I felt I should await the British reply to my appealing letter.

In all this uncertainty, I must admit that I nearly lost my nerve and cancelled the trip with Ludwig. The latter, very understandably, put out feelers to Fabian Geduldig, although he knew his holidays could only be half as long as ours. Meanwhile, on second thoughts I realized that if Martha did come to India she could not arrive before July and meanwhile her letters or telegrams could reach me wherever we set up our base camp. So, at the beginning of May, 1946, I set out northwards with all my worldly possessions. They were in three trunks. At the end of the trip I would have to label them again, either BOMBAY – or ENGLAND.

Though my attempts to obtain a travel permit for Gurla Mandhata had finally failed, we still hoped to be granted one for Rakaposhi, hence Ludwig, Fabian and I met in Lahore and from there went due north to Srinagar, instead of starting from Almora. In Srinagar, we told the authorities we were expecting a telegram from Delhi at any moment allowing us into Gilgit for our attempt on Rakaposhi. The official, an Englishman, listened politely to our story and said he would be glad to see us again when the telegram had arrived.

Meanwhile, we hired three bicycles and went shopping to lay in stores for the expedition. After that, there was time to look round. Apart from some large and hideous hotels, reminiscent of those built at the turn of the century at Interlaken or Bad Gastein, Srinagar, the capital of Kashmir, is a picturesque town set in beautiful surroundings. We had been told that Srinagar was the Venice of the East, but in the town itself the only waterways we could see were one or two narrow canals. As elsewhere, the inhabitants lived in solid houses on solid earth, while the bazaar with its dark alleyways was typical of others we had seen. Admittedly, there were some house-boats and people, including ourselves, lived in them because a patch of water was cheaper to rent than a plot of ground. All the same, the rent was high for our pockets, like the price of most things in Srinagar where there was a thriving tourist trade, and the inhabitants seemed to take a personal pride in coaxing extortionate sums from European and Indian visitors for Kashmir shawls, carved wooden cabinets, brassware, carpets and other souvenirs.

But there is a fairy-tale atmosphere about this part of the world which no commercialism can destroy. Our house-boat sat on the dark, motionless water of the canal overshadowed by huge tropical plane-trees. Occasionally a boat passed, sending ripples to slap against the hull and stirring the water-lilies in a nearby creek. Sometimes a melodious voice would call outside our little window: *"Dudh hai, dudh nahin mangta?"* "Milk? Do you not wish for milk?" Then boats laden with strawberries, cherries, flowers and the famous products of local craftsmanship, the hand-woven shawls and superb wood carvings, would come floating past.

Just outside Srinagar is a large shallow lake called the *Dal* where trim gondolas with brightly coloured sun-roofs ply for hire. One of them took us through broad canals flanked by primeval forest and out into the open water. There the traders descended on us like pirates waylaying a merchantman and for fifteen minutes or more they hovered round, appealing, beseeching, halving the price of their wares and then halving it again – all, of course, to no purpose, for we must have been among the most poverty-stricken mortals in all Kashmir.

When we reached the middle of the lake we dived into the luke-warm water and gazed round at the crescent of 14,000-foot and 16,000-foot mountains which surround the Kashmir Basin – a wide crescent, for the Basin is about eighty miles long. There is another lake at its northern end. Srinagar is 5,800 feet above sea-level and the high altitude, coupled with the protective wall of mountains, make the climate extremely equable with only moderate rainfall. The average temperature in January is several degrees above freezing and in July it is only 75°F, as compared with 99°F in the Indus Valley. Some idea of the summer heat in the Indian plains is given by these average temperatures which we worked out at an internment camp where the atmosphere was clear and dry, and we did not, in fact, feel the heat as particularly excessive: main water – 88°F; river water – 81°F; water cooled in an earthenware jug – 70°F. At this same camp, the lowest night temperature recorded was 71°F. No wonder many British people liked to retire to Kashmir after spending their working lives in India, or that apples, pears, peaches and cherries are hardly found elsewhere in India, but flourish in Kashmir!

Four-fifths of the population of Kashmir are Moslems and of the remainder, the most influential minority are the Hindus. If we had not already known this, we would have found out quickly enough when we came to buy provisions for our trip. Tinned meat, we discovered, was unobtainable, the pig being unclean to those of Islamic faith and the cow being a sacred animal of the Hindus.

Valuable time passed and no telegram arrived, so we prepared to leave for the area which Ludwig had selected as his third choice if both Gurla Mandhata and Rakaposhi failed. This was the Padar region lying about eighty miles downriver from Kailang. When we were on the point of starting, the telegram did arrive, but it made no difference to our plans as it merely said that if we wished to enter Gilgit for Rakaposhi next year, a permit would be issued!

An hour or two later we were in a lorry heading for the Chenab Valley. We had already been to the source of the river in 1939. With its 21,570 feet, the highest mountain in the region was slightly higher than Mulkila. The approach to it would also be longer and more laborious and the whole area larger and more highly glaciated than Lahul. The only mountaineering literature was the report of a courageous Englishwoman who had crossed the Umasi Pass in the previous year.

As the tight-packed truck went bumping and shuddering over the rough roads, we caught glimpses of an enchantingly domesticated landscape. The road climbed up to the rim of the Basin and from there the terraced paddy-fields – which are kept perpetually inundated – stretched away below us to the far horizon. After crossing the pass we descended in a series of tight curves with a sheer drop on one side. Even allowing for the twists in the road and the state of the surface, the driver seemed to us to be steering a very erratic course. Between the human forms huddled and draped all around us, we caught sight of the wretched man steering with two fingers while he fumbled about for a packet of cigarettes! We yelled to him to be careful; he yelled something back. Then the other passengers joined in, laughing, shouting at us, at him, at each other. Meanwhile, the lorry was driving itself.

We spent the night at Batote near the Chenab River and next day, as it proved impossible to get by bus to Doda as we had hoped, Ludwig and I climbed a short slope to get a view of the mountains we were aiming for. The sky was overcast and we could not see much, but glimpses of the Padar region through gaps in the clouds looked exciting.

An Evangelical missionary was kind enough to take charge of two of my three trunks which, as I have said, contained all my possessions. There were books, bed sheets, a city suit and some albums of music, none of which would be of much use to me in the Himalayas. I gave the missionary my treasured violin separately, asking him to take special care to keep it out of the damp. Once already, in the monsoons, it had disintegrated in the humid atmosphere and in that state had been presented to me by a fellow-internee in one of the camps. I had waited until the dry season returned and then stuck it together again.

Next morning, by dint of bribery and a good deal of shoving, Ludwig and Fabian succeeded in boarding the bus for Doda. I, on the other hand, walked there, a distance of nearly thirty miles, under the full glare of the tropic sun. By the time I reached Doda, the others had set up the tents for the night, got a meal ready and hired horses for the next stage in the journey as far as Kishtwar. The following morning the drover arrived with mules. As mules are slower than horses, that meant another half-day's march, but as we had no means of checking the man's story – something about his leading horse having fallen sick – we had to accept the situation.

For three days, we journeyed through varied scenery up the caravan route which followed the course of the Chenab River. As far as Kishtwar the area was inhabited, fields and villages lying on broad terraces on either side of the narrow valley. The oak was the principal tree. We failed to recognize it at first as, in this area, the oaks bear leaves with sharp thorns up to a height of six or nine feet from the ground. On the last day, just before we came to Kishtwar on its miniature plateau, the river dropped below us into a deep gorge while the road wound laboriously up and down the cliffs on either side. Here, we saw oleanders and in some places tall, straight-trunked Himalayan cedars. There were more splendid specimens growing in and around Kishtwar.

In a ravine behind one of the rest-houses we met a band of gypsies, fine-looking people with eloquent eyes. They were in the act of moving to another camp and had several horses with them, but so much baggage that men, women and children had to carry some of it themselves, mostly cooking utensils, including cauldrons and attractively engraved copper jugs which they balanced on their heads. I noticed that the women were richly adorned with silver ornaments.

When we reached Kishtwar on May 23, the drover sprang a surprise, demanding the same payment for his meandering mules as we had agreed on for horses. He said he was prepared to take our entire baggage back with him if we thought we could do better with somebody else. I seem to remember that we paid.

Further up beyond Kishtwar we found that the Chenab Valley was uninhabited and the route extremely difficult. With the help of a local official we unearthed two drovers who were prepared to transport our luggage on three horses and a donkey to Machail, which was five days' journey away. But they charged us a fearful price. We agreed to pay them a lump sum for the whole journey regardless of the time it took and so failed at first to understand why the two men wanted to halt and set up camp in the early afternoon of the first day. But when we tried to insist on marching for a further two hours we discovered the reason: they were afraid. Immediately ahead the pathway consisted of wooden planks wedged into the rocks, 2,000 or 3,000 feet above the river, and, beyond that, of steep and rickety steps over a sheer drop. Further still were steep slopes down which we had to slide with practically nothing at the bottom to stop us going over the edge. Each of our poor animals had to be led separately over the worst bits, but perhaps "led" is the wrong word; the leading horse, a really courageous beast, had to move at least some of the way on its own initiative or the others would never have followed. When the horse went uphill we pulled and pushed, and when downhill two of us hung on to his tail. And this went on for three whole days! On the return journey, instead of horses we had porters for this stretch, which was much more sensible.

Stiff climbs up the loveliest and wildest Alpine peaks convey very well what climbing is like in the Himalayas. But it is impossible to enjoy in Europe, even on camping and hiking holidays, the nomadic life such as one lives on the long marches to and from the mountains of Asia. Those days we spent in the valleys of the Chandra, the Bhaga and the Chenab were certainly strenuous, but do not most of the joys of mountaineering spring from the danger, hardship and toil which it involves?

Our two drovers were always careful to find us a good site for the nightly camp. Sometimes it would be a level patch of fine green grass, with a stream running nearby, or they would choose a certain spot because there was plenty of dry wood lying about for the camp fires. It was a wonderful moment when the site had been selected and one's shoulders were free at last of the abominable rucksack. But, before we could relax, there were various jobs to be done. We all had our own so that things worked smoothly almost without need of talk. While the drovers saw to their animals, collected fuel and made their own bivouac, Fabian, Ludwig and I usually began by getting out of our sweaty clothes and putting on pyjamas. Even when there was no water to wash in, or the water was too icily cold, it was a delectable feeling to slip into soft dry flannel after a long and hot day's march. If the evening got cold, we put on sweaters. One of us, Ludwig, say, would then fetch water, Fabian would get out the rice, salt and seasoning from the food-box, and meanwhile I would have lit two camp fires between six lumps of rock. Fabian would bring over the food and the cooking pots and, as I blew and poked and wiped the smoke from my eyes, the tent would be taking shape in a sheltered spot to windward and all made ready for the night: triple sleeping-bags put one inside the other and air-beds blown up.

Then, at last, we could settle down. Off would come the climbing boots to the enormous relief of one's toes; then warm slippers, and food. We ate out of the Indian equivalent of the mess-tin and saw to an ample supply of calories for the following day. We were always so hungry! Sometimes we would swap a few morsels with the drovers. Always we would finish supper with large quantities of tea.

For the rest of the evening we might sing songs or star-gaze under Ludwig's learned direction – so long as we did not have to stand up or turn round. Sometimes we just sat by the glowing fire, silent for minutes on end, each with his own thoughts, but all feeling replete and comfortably tired, with the faint smell of pine, smoke and horses drifting in the air. There would still be a gleam, perhaps, in the western sky, with a few trees silhouetted against it and stars caught in the black tracery of the branches. Soon the darkness would be complete and only a glow from the dying fires would touch familiar faces, suddenly remote in the dignity of repose.

An ornately carved wooden temple in the Bhut-Nadi, a tributary valley of the Chenab *(Fabian Geduldig)*

And so it was on this occasion, on the last stage before Atholi, with the added joy of the river roaring over the rocks, far below us and invisible, the sound reaching us as a faint rumble overlaying the silence of a region where not a village, not a hut, not a human being existed for miles.

* * * *

To reach Machail from Atholi we followed a steep side-valley of the Chenab called the Bhut-Nadi, where a tributary surged down over the rocks, throwing up clouds of spray. But the valley was actually broader and more friendly than that of the main river with villages and farms, many of them with richly carved façades, spread along its length. In some places we saw high-gabled wooden Hindu temples, picturesquely sited, though surprisingly the trees in the district reminded us of home: walnut, cherries, oaks, poplars, limes, firs and pines, besides the tall, strong Himalayan cedar.

We slept at the end of the first day's march in a recently built rest-house in Chishote. The evening meal was memorable: buttermilk followed by fragrant elder flowers picked during the day and now dipped in flour and water and fried in oil.

We reached Machail on May 29. Though we were now eight days' journey beyond the end of the negotiable road we found a police-post there, reason: sapphire mines in a nearby mountain. The police chief promised to help us recruit porters, but told us it was useless to try at the moment as all the able-bodied men would be setting off next day over the Umasi La to fetch salt from Zaskar. Every summer for the last 3,000 years the people of

A farmhouse in the Bhut-Nadi *(Fritz Kolb)*

Machail have performed this journey, herding hundreds of sheep over the 17,370-foot glacier pass to have them sheared in Zaskar and, in payment for the wool, to receive salt which the Zaskaris obtain from the lakes beyond the Himalayas. It would be three weeks, said the policeman, before the men returned.

As there was no rest-house at Machail we set up our tent and, that done, started out again southwards with a villager as guide to climb to a point on Agyásol (20,400 feet) from which our main objective, an unnamed mountain, 21,570 feet high, on longitude 76° 8′ E and north latitude 33° 37′, could be seen. Before long, the guide lost his way and landed us in a dense thicket of alders. Crawling out, we took over the lead ourselves and by dusk had found the right path again, just in time to reach a pair of empty huts where we could spend the night. Each hut contained one small, low-ceilinged room beneath a roof of horizontal beams on which rested a layer of earth, 18 inches thick with grass growing on the top. The huts were identical, but as one room would be too small for four people, we took over the first and told Gangaram, the guide, to sleep in the second. We said goodnight and he went off to the adjoining hut. Then, after some time, he came back, or rather crept back into our crowded bedroom. We asked him what was the matter. He said he could not sleep in the other hut. Why? He said he was afraid of "the spirits". We were too sleepy to argue and, anyway, we did not want to upset him, so we let him stay. Then, suddenly, at about one o'clock, there was a terrific crash. We rushed outside and saw that the roof of the other but had collapsed, dropping a ton or more of earth into the empty room. If Gangaram had been there he would certainly have been killed.

High up under the rock walls of Agyásol we sat on a hump of snow to examine the *terra incognita*. It certainly included some lordly mountains! They were steeper and looked more forbidding than the mountains of Lahul; their height from valley to summit was greater, and no less than eight 20,000-foot peaks were visible from our vantage point: first Agyásol itself, a magnificently shaped peak, but extremely austere, then, directly facing us, another of 20,440 feet with a flank so steep that the most famous of the Alpine walls would have looked tame in comparison, and, above the Barnaj Valley, three more fine peaks. One of them was too steep to carry snow and Ludwig christened it Baleful Barnaj, saying frankly that he had no desire to attempt it. The mountain next to it was called Shivji ka Pahar, the Mountain of Shiva, the local inhabitants believing that the god Shiva had selected it as his dwelling so as to be safe from all intruders. The mountains visible to us stood in a half-circle with our objective (denoted as SM. 21,570 on the map, p.91) in the centre. It was thickly covered with ice and, though too shapeless to be called beautiful, was undoubtedly king among its neighbours and very difficult to climb. It had two peaks; the nearer with a curious ice-field shaped like a sickle moon, as though pasted over it. It seemed not to possess a local name. Whenever we asked we were told *"Do nali"*, which merely means "two valleys" and referred to the fork in the valley leading up to it. Amongst ourselves we called the mountain The Sickle Moon.

The summit of The Sickle Moon and, right, neighbouring peaks *(Fabian Geduldig)*

We set up our base camp at the fork in the valley and got a straggling bunch of old men and boys to carry our luggage there. Keeping back Gangaram and his friend, Shivdyal, as servants and porters, we then set out to find The Sickle Moon. At first, we thought it was merely a matter of finding a suitable approach, but after some days we realized that the problem was to find the mountain itself: somehow it had got lost. We had all seen it from Agyásol directly above the site where we now had our camp. Since then, we had scrambled about in every direction without catching so much as a glimpse. This is what happened:

June 4, 1946. Ludwig and Fabian climbed up to about 16,000 feet on a mountain above the north branch of the valley – no sign of The Sickle Moon. Meanwhile I explored the west branch and found it heavily glaciated. I saw some splendid mountains, but "ours" was not among them. But for lack of time I could not get to the head of the glacier. From there, perhaps, some gap might have led to The Sickle Moon.

June 5 and 6. Ludwig and Fabian decided to scale the mountain immediately above the camp, where the valley forked. They climbed the first day, bivouacked for the night and were nearing the summit on the second day when they came to unexpected obstacles and had to turn back – without sighting The Sickle Moon. During that time I explored the first three or four miles of the north branch of the valley, then a sharp pain in my knee forced me to return to camp and take a day's rest.

June 7 and 8. Ludwig followed my tracks up the north valley and bivouacked at the point where I had turned back. Next day he climbed up a glacier to a mountain of about 18,700 feet, which he nicknamed The Cornerstone. The weather was poor and having struggled to the ridge, he could see nothing below him on the other side but a gigantic glacier with steep slopes rising from it below the mist. Thinking they might be the lower slopes of The Sickle Moon, he continued to climb in the hope of seeing more, but higher up he found deep snow and, being alone, could not go on to the summit.

Back at the camp we sifted this scanty information, but could extract nothing definite. No answer was forthcoming, either, from the conjunction of bearings which we had taken from various points, no answer to the question: what had happened to the mountain which we had all seen ten days before?

However, the week was not unrelieved disappointment. Our base camp was such a homely place that we always felt glad to return to it. Apart from its ideal site at the spot where the valley forked – ideal, because we still did not know which of the two branches would lead us to our mountain – its height of slightly over 12,000 feet, though rather low as a starting-point for climbing, made it much more convenient to live in than a site higher up. All the wood we needed for the camp fires was within thirty minutes' reach, so we could save our seven pints of paraffin for later use in the higher camps. The young shoots of succulent ferns growing among the debris of the moraine served as fresh vegetables, and a type of cress, also growing nearby, as salad. Finally, there was a clear spring which provided unlimited water.

We were not called upon to be vegetarians, either. We had bought a sheep for fifteen rupees and in due course made a wonderful soup with lumps of meat floating in it. Unfortunately, we had to share the remainder of the sheep with some small beast of prey that burrowed down one night through the frozen snow to where the treasure lay hidden. What remained had again to be shared with large numbers of maggots that found refrigeration no bar to enterprise.

Bread, or the equivalent, was our worst problem. At his school in Udaipur, Ludwig had pretty well mastered the art of making *chapátis* and, if we had been able to get hold of the black wheaten flour called *atta* of which they are usually made, all would have been well. But we could only buy grain. Gangaram had ground it in a hand-mill for us before leaving Machail, but what a mill! And what a result! The stuff he brought us looked more like coarse sand than flour or grits. I made a sieve out of a cheese carton and he and I worked for hours trying to extract the finer particles. But even those were useless for *chapátis*. We could not bring ourselves to throw away the grain left in the sieve, so we soaked it in water overnight and next day made porridge with it. The "flour" I ultimately baked into a kind of crispbread and it went down well in the higher camps where we drank a lot of tea.

Apart from spices, we found copra an excellent flavouring. As we had no mortar, we ground it between two stones and there was always a large indigestible residue. But the fat content and the delicate aroma came in useful when we made curry.

Though a height of 12,000 feet was very moderate for the Himalayas, the rarefied atmosphere meant that vegetables and fruit took longer to cook. During the march to the base camp, for instance, we cooked some beans, but they were so hard as to be almost inedible and were returned to the rucksack for a later occasion. They improved slightly after a second cooking, but were still not popular, and again the left-overs went with us on the following day's march. That evening, by common consent, we dumped them in some nettles at the back of a rest-house.

But I meant to say more about the camp site. It was one of those delightfully level triangles often found as the product of slow erosion at the confluence of rivers or glaciers. Half of the site was still covered with frozen snow, the rest was a carpet of soft grass dotted, when we arrived, with hundreds of white, star-like flowers. A week later, blue ones had taken their place; later still red ones. Once before, in 1939, we had pitched our tents in such a triangle, but then the base had been dominated by slate cliffs continually liable to fall on us, whereas here there was merely a sloping meadow with boulders. On one of these a small bird came and perched every morning and it would sound foolish if I tried to describe the nostalgia its call awakened: cuck-oo! cuck-oo!

Our "camp" consisted of a single four-man tent. Gangaram and Shivdyal slept further down in a cave which the *gaddis* – the nomad shepherds – had made habitable by building a wall of stones in front and spreading dry rhododendron foliage on the floor. Later, the *gaddis* arrived with their herds and some of them slept in the cave, to the great relief of our two porters, whose nights had been haunted by the fear of bears ever since we had seen fresh tracks on the west glacier.

For cooking we had carefully designed and built a hearth of stones in which we used two fires simultaneously, any heat escaping between them being effectively utilized by an extremely light, dome-shaped aluminium kettle.

How lovely those evenings were, when the fires blazed and the stars glittered, when Agyásol reared, broad-based, from the valley, its peak seeming to pierce the Milky Way! Crawling into the tent, we would light the candles and there, pinned to the tentpole, would be the photograph of my wife climbing with Ludwig's fiancée, taken just before we left Austria in 1939. Now it was 1946. Soon, perhaps, my wife and I would be together again. But I had had no word from her yet.

*   *   *   *

Fabian's holiday would soon be over and we had not yet climbed a mountain to the summit. We were determined to do so before he had to leave us and we chose a fine looking mountain of about 19,200 feet which we had seen from Agyásol among those clustering round The Sickle Moon and from which we hoped we might catch another glimpse of it. We called it the Trihedron, but after reaching the summit with two intermediate caps on June 12, we changed the name to Fabian's Peak. The climb gave us a certain sense of achievement as there was very steep snow throughout, the standing room on the summit was extremely small and the last part of the climb led over huge cornices. But above all, we at last saw The Sickle Moon again, a gigantic mass rearing skywards in the same ridge as ourselves, but with three intervening peaks. So we had not been the victims of a hallucination after all, but we had grossly underestimated the distances and, as a result, had failed to notice that there were other mountains between us and our objective.

The Sickle Moon was clearly a worthwhile goal, and Ludwig and I still had plenty of time to attempt it. But the problem remained: How to get there? From where we stood on Fabian's Peak the head of the West Donali Glacier was hidden in cloud so

The view from below Trihedron and at the summit *(Fritz Kolb)*

we still could not tell whether a pass led from there to our mountain. Far below us to eastward, Ludwig recognized the huge glacier which he had first seen some days before from The Cornerstone. It flowed north and he maintained that it was the top part of the East Donali Glacier, which could be reached from the north branch of the fork in the valley where we had our base camp. All we had to do, he claimed, was to keep going and eventually the glacier would lead round the foot of The Cornerstone and straight up to the slopes of The Sickle Moon.

That might be so, but if we tried that approach and Ludwig turned out to be wrong we would have wasted an awful lot of time. So we decided to explore the head of the West Donali Glacier first and, if that failed, to test Ludwig's theory later.

While Fabian was on his journey back, Ludwig and I were spending an entire night shaking the snow from our tent as it fell, thick and fast, on the West Donali Glacier. Somewhere in the neighbourhood, but fortunately not too close, we could hear avalanches thundering down into the valley. The next morning brought no change in the weather, but we had a diversion. Intending to make semolina soup, Ludwig poured salt instead of semolina into the boiling water. The salt bag was now empty and to get more would mean a two-day journey. But we rallied to the crisis in the best Scouting style and simply boiled off the water until only the salt remained.

It went on snowing for the rest of that day and on through the night until the following morning, when a biting frost set in. Through the walls of the tent it came, penetrated the outer sleeping-bags of sail-cloth, cut through the inner quilting, seeped through our clothes and froze our skins. But the weather had cleared. Daylight came an hour earlier than on the previous day and above the surrounding rock-walls we saw white puff-ball clouds sailing across a deep blue sky.

Yet, the question nearly remained unanswered. We had not got much further beyond the point where I had turned back the week before when, softened by the sun, the ice crust began to give way beneath our feet and with every step we were sinking up to the waist in snow. Obviously, if this went on we would never cover the remaining two miles or so to the head of the glacier. In a long mountaineering career I have never felt so helpless as at that moment. It looked as though we would be forced to turn back and try the East Donali Glacier. But, if that failed, there would be no time for a second attempt in the west and all thought of The Sickle Moon would have to be abandoned with the nagging suspicion that we might have got through on the West Glacier after all.

But it seemed we would have no choice and would have to turn back until, a few hundred yards ahead of us on the right side of the valley, we saw the trail of a recent avalanche. Avalanche snow is hard and we knew we could probably climb it and perhaps get a view of the head of the glacier from the top. The difficulty was to reach the avalanche. We struggled on through the soft snow, leaving a veritable trench behind us, until at last we floundered up on to 'a hard, bumpy surface and then climbed quite easily to the top of the avalanche. From there, we could indeed see into the farthest corner of the glacier. It was sealed off by high walls, or rock. Clearly there was no access to our mountain from that side.

Two days later Ludwig succeeded in persuading our two timorous porters to lug a tent, food supplies and fuel up to a massive block of granite sitting like a giant's throne high up on the ice of the East Donali Glacier. Here we set up our base for putting Ludwig's theory to the test. Just above us the glacier turned sharp west, to head, as he maintained, round The Cornerstone mountain to the foot of The Sickle Moon.

A crust of ice had formed over the new snow and for the time being the danger of avalanches receded. It looked as though by evening we might have found out whether The Sickle Moon could be reached from the West Donali Glacier *(Ludwig Krenek)*

This time we made a good resolution. We intended from now on to abandon that bad habit (by no means uncommon among Himalayan climbers) of starting late for the day's climb. Long ago, when reading expedition reports at home, I had noticed that Himalayan mountaineers did not always exercise that iron discipline which Alpine guides impose on their parties with such an astonishing effect on the daily distance climbed. Whether starting from the Trift Hotel for the Rothorn, from the Weisshornhütte for the Weisshorn, or from the Grands Mulets for Mont Blanc, tourists are faced with a climb of between 5,000 and 6,000 feet and the guides put them through it – even the weaker brethren – quite easily in one day by starting at two or three o'clock in the morning.

Almost thirty years ago, on my very first climb in the West Alps, I learnt what a lot of trouble, disappointment and danger a late start can entail, and ever since, to my great profit, I have followed the example of the Alpine guides, particularly on difficult routes which are not much frequented. In the Himalayas, an early start to the day is doubly advisable because the climb is bound to take longer than a comparable ascent in the Alps. Firstly, the terrain will be unfamiliar. Secondly, the larger numbers usually taking part in a Himalayan climb will inevitably delay the start. Cooking and dressing in a tent instead of in an Alpine hut will also require more time and, incidentally, be much less pleasant. Lastly, if, as is likely, the men are not fully acclimatized to the high altitude, the smallest exertion will make them short of breath and slow them down. In short, more time will be needed all round. An earlier start will supply this and bring extra benefits. It may be unnecessary, for instance, to set up intermediate camps. Soft snow and the danger from avalanches which occur later in the day will be avoided and, possibly, the ordeal of intolerable heat. Often the dangers accompanying a deterioration in the weather can also be foreseen in time to be avoided.

At heights up to 23,000 feet, human beings can become so well adapted to the reduced atmospheric pressure that normal climbing speeds can be more or less maintained. Once acclimatized, the mountaineer has really no excuse for late starting. As long ago as 1907, Dr. Longstaff showed what can be achieved in one day when he climbed Trisul from a camp nearly 6,000 feet below the summit.

I admit that the situation may be different at heights approaching 26,000 feet. In these extreme cases, the human organism often refuses to adapt itself completely and the mountaineer is in a state of chronic hebetude. If that is so, an inordinate effort may be needed to leave the tent at all, and he is more likely to make it in daylight than at two in the morning when the wind howls and batters the tent and the stars, twinkling through the driving snow, far from encouraging him, merely serve as a reminder that a slight increase in the wind-force or a momentary attack of giddiness may be enough to transfer him to the next world. But though this may apply in the highest regions, they can only be reached from the lower contours of 16,000, 19,000 and 20,000 feet and at these intermediate heights I am convinced that well-led expeditions will come more and more to copy the example of the Alpine guides and start early in the day, instead of continuing the laborious and dangerous practice of working their way up a mountain with many, far too many, bivouacs.

In our camp on the East Donali Glacier we had but little occasion to put these principles into practice; but we did what was possible. First, at Ludwig's insistence, we abolished the usual breakfast before starting and substituted tea stirred into a mixture of glucose and roasted *sattu*, or barley-corn. To cook and eat this concoction took only a quarter of an hour and we found it palatable, easily digestible and reasonably satisfying. As there were only two of us and we got everything ready the night before, we did succeed in this way in leaving camp at an Alpine hour. We stopped for our first proper meal when we were quite high up, when the first rays of sun began to warm us – if the sun was shining. Then we brought out a pot of cold rice or porridge.

We were always back at the tent before nightfall, though sometimes only by dint of the perpetual jog-trot which we had perfected as internees at Dehra Dun. To slake the thirst which plagued us after such a day we drank tea and also our own special brew which we made from ginger crushed between two stones and dropped into hot, not necessarily boiling, water and allowed to draw, with brown Indian sugar added.

Despite bad weather we started our reconnaissance the morning after we had set up camp. Disappointment was soon forthcoming: the glacier did not continue round the foot of The

Cornerstone, but came to an end a little higher up in semicircular slate walls. Next day we climbed the west part of the wall and found at last the answer to the question: was The Sickle Moon mountain approachable from this side? It was. Two adjoining snow passes led without visible obstacles to the huge glacier basin above which towered the mountain.

North of both passes stood another mountain which we tried to climb at once so as to get a better view of the area, but the weather suddenly deteriorated and we had to turn back. Two days later we made another attempt in good weather and reached the summit (19,000 feet). There was not a cloud in the sky. The sunshine poured on us where we stood in the little enclave we had hacked out of the snow of the topmost cornice. We could photograph, survey and gaze our fill on the splendid panorama of peaks.

Now that we had a real bird's-eye view of the area, we saw that its geography was quite different from the impression we had formed. An illustration will help to explain how this had come about. Two tourists, say, are on the outskirts of a city. Right in the centre amongst the houses they can see the spire of the Cathedral which they intend to visit. They consult a rough, small-scale map which they have brought with them and find that the street where they are standing should lead straight to it. So they set off and after an hour or so's walk reach the heart of the city. They can no longer see the Cathedral, but know it must be somewhere close by, probably to their left, a few hundred yards off the main street. They look for a turning and here, sure enough, is just what they would expect to find – a side-alley at right angles to the street. They turn off, but the alley is a dead-end, so they try the next one, another dead-end. Then they ask a passer-by. He smiles and says: "I expect you are beginning to wonder if the Cathedral has vanished suddenly? I'll show you ...", and he takes them to an attic window in his house. There, so close they could almost touch it, is the spire again, rising in all its splendour above the roof-tops. But to reach the Cathedral, the man explains, they will have to go back the way they have come and enter the city from a different side!

The natural way to reach The Sickle Moon mountain would be to climb up the Prul Valley from Kishtwar. The existing map shows the Prul Glacier as quite small, whereas it is one of the biggest, if not the biggest, in the whole area. Its huge bulk runs from the main ridge stretching between Nun (23,410 feet) and the Hagshu Pass to the Padar group of mountains, which includes The Sickle Moon and a number of other high peaks.

Though considerably higher and more rugged than the main ridge, the Padar group is only a secondary ridge of many branches. We were sitting on one of its first peaks. Not far to the east would be the point where the crest joined the main ridge. To westward we could see the two passes we had just discovered, then Ludwig's Cornerstone, our Trihedron and more rugged peaks around the West Donali Glacier. Beyond those, the ridge divided, the south branch swinging up to Brammah (21,275 feet), while the north branch bore The Sickle Moon. According to existing surveys, this mountain is king of the Himalayas between Nun and an unnamed peak of 21,760 feet in Kulu, 150 miles further east.

Far below us, at the north foot of the great mountain, lay one of those magnificently flat ice-fields often found at the junction of several broad glaciers. Green-flecked lateral moraines surrounded by unexplored passes and unclimbed peaks seemed to invite us to set up camp there. But, alas, we had no time. Those joys would be for others.

We called the 19,000-foot mountain which had given us such a splendid view of the region "Solstice Peak", because we climbed it on June 21. It would not have tempted us from a mountaineering point of view as both its shape and its slopes seemed unremarkable, but even on our first attempt we found rock and ice-work of a kind seldom encountered on normal routes in the Alps. Next day we climbed through steep snow gullies to avoid these difficulties and did not reach the ridge until we were higher up. Then, as so often in the Himalayas, we saw that the apparently harmless mountain was going to demand real skill. I remember particularly the trouble we had in circumventing an aiguille over a dangerous and difficult ice-shoulder. It was bad enough on the way up, but we realized that whoever was leader on the descent would risk setting the entire mass of old soft snow in motion and, falling with it, be left dangling in space. And sure enough, it happened to Ludwig. But from where he swung on the end of the rope he managed to catch on and then work his way up to the lower edge of the ridge. From

We called the 19,000-foot mountain, which had given us such a magnificent view of the region, Solstice Peak because we climbed it on June 21 *(Ludwig Krenek)*

there he made me a safeguard, now doubly essential, while I traversed down. In the gullies we had climbed to reach the ridge, a touch with the shaft of the ice-axe had been enough to start frightening avalanches of wet snow, and our experience as a whole taught us that this is many times more likely to happen in the Himalayas, with the snow of the pre-monsoon period, than with summer snow in the Alps.

The Sickle Moon mountain rears like some strange monster, head and shoulders above its neighbours. It has two peaks, one sharp-pointed of rock, and the other dome-shaped of ice. To

We could photograph, survey and gaze our fill on the splendid panorama as seen from
the summit of Solstice Peak *(Ludwig Krenek)*

The Sickle Moon rears like some strange monster, head and shoulders above its neighbours *(Ludwig Krenek)*

eastwards, the two peaks form a single wall of ice and rock which one would only attempt if the other flanks offered nothing easier. The ice-field, shaped like a sickle moon, lies near the top of the south peak. Whether or how it can be reached remains to be seen. From our unfavourable viewpoint on the Trihedron the west flanks appeared to be the most promising line of attack. Ludwig, who has interpreted our survey data and drawn a map of the Padar region, considers the north peak to be the higher.

Brammah (21,275 feet) and its eastward rival of 20,440 feet are roughly similar in shape to the Grandes Jorasses of the Mont Blanc group. The Barnaj Valley contains two neighbouring ice-peaks of about 20,800 feet, both extremely beautiful and, no doubt, very difficult to climb. Slightly to one side stands "Baleful

Barnaj", the mountain which Ludwig found so overawing. Another and lower peak in the Barnaj Valley has an uncanny resemblance to the Matterhorn. Beyond the Prul Glacier, a second more compact range of mountains containing fewer separate peaks stretches from Nun and Kun in Kashmir to the Hagshu Pass north-east of Machail. In his collection of photographs, Ludwig gave a tall, soft-contoured dome in this range the provisional title of "The Highest", for he thinks it may well be higher than The Sickle Moon.

I have already mentioned the mountain called Shivji ka Pahar, the Abode of Shiva. The ascent might be attempted from the south-east over a steep granite enclave. If this route proved impossible, the much more rugged approach up the north-west ridge would have to be attempted.

Agyásol, a mountain of extraordinary beauty, covers about the same area as an entire group of mountains in the Austrian Alps, the Schober Group, for instance, in the Hohe Tauern. Agyásol is three and a half miles from the village of Machail. Its total height is 20,400 feet. To reach the summit would probably to extremely difficult, but at this stage in our trip neither Ludwig nor I could say for certain. We were soon to find out.

* * * *

Ludwig and I now had a hard decision to make. Should we continue to explore means of climbing The Sickle Moon mountain, or would it be better to admit defeat and do something else in the time that remained?

By failing to use the Prul Valley approach from Kishtwar we had got to the wrong side of the mountain. That was the price we had to pay for clearing up some of the geography of the area. All the same, our discovery of the new passes opened up possibilities of an approach from Machail and this may turn out to be the most favourable route for the transport of equipment and supplies. But, from where we were, we should need two camps at least, and probably three, to get to the north or west side of the mountain, so it would be impossible to reach the summit without porters. Our own two sprightly servants could not be persuaded to go more than a couple of hours' walk from their cave at the Base Camp and it was useless to think of trusting them to bring up supplies. Having wasted so much time already, we could not contemplate shuttling to and fro ourselves with food and equipment for the climb. There remained these alternatives: either we could attack the mountain from the east flank, which was the nearest but also the most difficult, or else we could abandon the idea of climbing it at all.

Ludwig and I had arranged that he would make decisions affecting reconnaissance and survey, and I would have the last word in regard to the mountains to be climbed, from the point of view of the risks involved. The east flank of The Sickle Moon was certainly not unclimbable; I knew that after inspecting it closely from Solstice Peak. But it was undeniably dangerous, because the steepest part of the flank was more than 20,000 feet above sea-level and because of the likelihood of avalanches. Moreover, we would have to climb down over the same wall. The slightest mishap – breaking an ice-axe, for instance – might well seal our fate. And if we did have an accident, no one would be able to help us, no one would come up to see what had happened. We would not even be missed. I thought the idea foolhardy, and called it off.[7]

Meanwhile I had heard from London that my wife would join me in India. She was due to arrive in the middle of July. That meant I had at the most ten days before starting from Machail for Bombay. What could Ludwig and I do in that time?

"I'm for a go at Agyásol," said Ludwig from where he lay, face down on his air-bed, chewing currants. The day was over, we had carefully buttoned up the tent-flap and lit the candle.

We noted Agyásol as one possibility; then we discussed another. The map showed four passes leading from Machail over the main Himalayan chain to Zaskar, in the state of Kashmir. We believed that only one pass, the Umasi La, had so far been used by Europeans. I now suggested that we cross by one unexplored pass, tour Zaskar from end to end, and return to Machail by another unexplored pass.

Until the middle of the nineteenth century Zaskar had belonged to Tibet, and in faith, language and race the Zaskaris are, to this day, Tibetans, while in scenery, altitude and climate the region they inhabit is indistinguishable from its eastern neighbour. To visit Zaskar was, in all but political fact, to visit

---

[7] The first successful ascent of The Sickle Moon was made by an Indian expedition of the High Altitude Warfare School in 1975. The height is quoted at 6574 metres (21,694 ft)

Tibet, and Tibet I had always longed to see. But, quite rightly, Ludwig looked sceptical when I first suggested the idea, for it was unusual in a number of ways. Perhaps only mountaineers can appreciate this fully, but anyone can see that "touring" unknown country involves special risks and problems. In this case it would be like climbing up some Alpine valley, except that there would be no villages, roads, railways, tracks, huts and, above all, practically no people, and the mountain ridges would have to be raised to 16,000 or 19,000 feet. Peaks and passes would be known only from hearsay. Many Alpinists have carried a ten or twelve days' supply of food with them. Yet it is doubtful whether even they can imagine what it means to carry such a load – with a tent and sleeping-bag in addition – over trackless wastes of rock and ice at an altitude of 16,000 feet above sea-level. But this is what we would have to do, if Ludwig accepted my idea. The whole trip would have to be done in a strictly limited time and without porters – just as if, in fact, we were at home, following well beaten tracks on a hiking holiday.

Of course, if it had not been for my burning desire to see a former part of Tibet I would never have put forward this plan and I was not surprised when, despite his perennial thirst for adventure, Ludwig started raising objections. "It's impossible without porters," he said flatly. But we both knew we should never find anyone in Machail prepared to keep up on the forced marches I envisaged, so I tried to talk Ludwig round.

"We'll live like the natives," I said. "When they travel, they spend the night under the last birches on one side of a pass, cross it next day with a forced march and sleep by the first juniper bushes they come to on the far side. We need not take the Primus with us; we can rely on finding something to make a fire. And we need not lug the air-beds along – we shan't be pitching the tent on snow.

"But look at this map!" said Ludwig. "There is a pass here marked 'Old Deserted Road'. How can you be sure of getting that behind you in a day? Why is the road deserted? Perhaps because the glaciers have broken up and are impassable. And don't forget, this map was drawn nearly a hundred years ago!"

That was all perfectly true. But I persisted. "Well, we can take a packet of Meta tablets then, to be on the safe side. But one night on the ice without an air-bed won't kill us."

"We have got to be sure of having fuel of some kind," continued Ludwig. "We have got no bread, remember. We shall have to rely on rice and semolina to give us bulk – and they have got to be cooked. If we take no fuel with us and we don't come to your juniper bushes by nightfall, we shall have to go without supper or breakfast. And there's another thing ..."

That night we talked over the whole idea in detail. We discussed the pros and cons of every item of equipment and eventually reduced the load we should be carrying to the barest possible minimum. Even then it was enormous.

For me, all the same, the whole project remained just on the right side of the borderline between the possible and the impossible. Ludwig, on the other hand, was not yet ready to admit it was even feasible, though I could see he was weakening. At heart he was no less keen for the adventure than I. But meanwhile neither of us wanted to rush a decision and there was plenty to occupy us – first and foremost, our own domestic comfort. By midnight, as usual, our leaky air-beds had become deflated and we were feeling the cold in our hip bones. So we blew them up again, and repeated the process at intervals for the rest of the night. But in the morning, as usual, there was a hollow under each bed where the warmth of our bodies had melted the ice.

That day we struck camp and returned to Machail. On the day after, I reconnoitred Agyásol while Ludwig took photographs and did survey work on a peak near Machail. We returned to the village tired, sun-scorched, but with plenty to talk about. Ludwig had seen a bear chasing a sheep. "I would never have thought a bear could move so fast," he said. "The shepherds yelled, but it had no effect. Finally, the sheep made a desperate jump over a low wall of rock and somehow managed to get back to the flock. Then the bear gave up."

I, too, had a story to tell. I had been in an area almost a day's march from the nearest settlement. I had been climbing a hill when I noticed a solitary hut standing on a spur. Getting nearer, I could see that people lived there, though at the moment there was no sign of life. Then, as I was passing the hut, a woman came out with a child in her arms. When she saw me she stopped; then, to my surprise, she came running towards me. "Look!" she said. "Look!" – and showed me her baby. It was dead. "He has suddenly died," she said, " – and I don't know why ...." That was all. There was nothing I could say to comfort the woman, though

Agyásol. It was a beautiful, a really splendid mountain, a 20,000-footer *(Ludwig Krenek)*

there was no need to see her face or hear her voice to know that she was distraught. How, otherwise, could she have spoken to me, a stranger, and a white man, at that, when all her own people were away?

I then told Ludwig about Agyásol. "It will be a tough climb. To start with there is a high ice wall, and pretty steep, something like the Brenva flank on Mont Blanc. The wall leads to a shoulder on a ridge. We should need an intermediate camp there. Then we should have to cross the ridge. I could not see what it was like on the other side, except that it leads up to a fantastically rough glacier. Somewhere from the top of that would be the approach to the summit. We should have a very lively finale, I can assure you."

"How much time do you think we should need?"

"Four to five days."

There was a pause. Ludwig looked at me; I looked at Ludwig. Then, quite naturally, the conversation reverted to the Zaskar plan, with the double crossing of the main Himalayan chain.

It was at Dartse in 1939 that I had first felt the lure of Inner Asia, felt drawn to that magic world almost physically, as iron is drawn to a magnet. But then there had been no choice. We had set out to climb the highest peak in Lahul and had only one possible goal – Mulkila and its neighbours. But now, in 1946, we were not tied to any fixed programme. It was entirely up to us: Agyásol or Zaskar.

But though Ludwig and I had free choice, it was still a difficult one, for the reason, basically, that we wanted to climb Agyásol *and* explore Zaskar, but only had time to do one. And this might be the last, the very last, time we had a chance to do either. So the debate was resumed .... The case for Agyásol: it was a beautiful, a really splendid mountain, a 20,000-footer, and so far on this trip we had climbed no mountain of that height. As against that, there was no denying the similarity between one mountain and another. In essence Agyásol was no different from so many other large lumps of rock, ice and snow we had climbed in the past, except that it was even larger. But to see something of Tibet would be quite new; that would mean more to me than anything Agyásol could offer. I knew what I wanted, but was honestly prepared to forgo it if Ludwig was not in favour. So it was up to him.

Caution is the quality that keeps mountaineers alive, but Ludwig was not only, or even chiefly, a mountaineer. He had both inherited and earned the titles of explorer and geographer. He had crossed the African continent from Cape Town to Cairo, on the way climbing among the Drakensberg Mountains and reaching the summits of Kibo and Mavensi, and he had explored Lasistan in Turkey. Is it surprising that during these last days he, too, had heard the siren-song of Inner Asia? The thirst for new horizons finally overcame all his objections, valid as they were. He had just lit the candle in the tent and was carefully sticking it with melted wax on to a stone when I heard him say: "As regards cameras, we'll just take yours – it's lighter ...." Ludwig had decided for Zaskar.

For Ludwig to forego his own camera on an occasion like this was a truly heroic decision. I fully realized that. And I also sensed that his dramatic pronouncement was intended to symbolize the fact that we were in for something out of the ordinary.

That same night, late as it was, we started packing.

CHAPTER 4

Last Fling

THE map shows four passes leading from the Padar region of Kashmir to Zaskar. They are named, running from north-east to south-east, the Hagshu La, the Umasi La, the Muni La and the Poat La. The last was the most tempting geographically, but it was too far east for us to reach it in time. A British woman explorer had crossed the Umasi La in the previous year and fully described it, so we decided to cross the Muni La on the way out and return by the Hagshu La. According to the map, the Muni La was no longer in use. Our two porters helped us carry the rucksacks as far as Bujwas, where we discharged them.

Ludwig then recalled that in Bujwas there was said to be living an old man famed throughout the region for his accurate knowledge of the mountains. We asked our way to his house and were told there that he was away, but would be back in a few days. At the time this news did not strike us as particularly fateful, but in fact the whole trip would have taken a very different course if we had possessed first-hand, up-to-date knowledge from the start, instead of having to rely on the conjectures of the only available map of the region, which was drawn over 100 years ago. But the trip had only just begun and the total load of about 110 pounds which we carried on our backs failed to outweigh our enthusiasm. There, beyond the white mountains, we told each other, lay mysterious Tibet, the land of telepathy, prayer-flags, Buddhist monasteries and crystal-clear air. On the very next day we thought we would be standing on the pass, at the gateway to the object of our boyhood dreams. Of course, besides a residue of youthful romanticism it was the sober desire for knowledge that lured us on, allied to elements of the mysticism that during our long stay in India had gradually taken root in our shrunken souls. For some reason, at any rate, we were full of a strange euphoria, confident that we were heading for a kind of Blessed Land and prepared to pay almost any price to see it.

But late on that first afternoon we encountered a snag. The route we had been following turned left suddenly to climb a steep slope, skirt a shoulder and so enter the side-valley leading up to the Umasi La. It was, in fact, the direct route to that pass. We, on the other hand, wanted the main valley, on the far side of the Umasi River. But we could find no means of crossing it. There were no bridges and no fords. In several places, great granite blocks divided the stream into separate torrents, but the gaps were all too wide to jump. We were beginning to think we were stuck when, further up the valley, we came to a broad natural bridge where we could cross dry-shod and without difficulty. By that time, night was coming on. There were faint traces of what might have been paths on the far side of the river leading on to a wooded moraine which we had chosen from a distance as our camp-site.

Birch wood burns slowly and easily goes out. But in this part of the Himalayas the birch climbs higher than any other tree and those travelling with such simple means as we were must always look on it as a friend. It supplies fuel for their camp-fire on the way up to a pass and is the first tree to greet them when they come down again. To us, the "last birches" and the "first birches" were the two havens between which lay a perilous waste-land.

That night, as we levelled the ground among the birches on the moraine, on our way to the Muni La, we broke the shaft of an ice-axe. Throughout the war, the axes we had with us in 1939 had lain in the attic of a building in Lahore, and when I collected them in 1946, many of the shafts had become so desiccated that I could snap them easily over my knee. This one had survived – until now. A bad omen? Nonsense! That night and for most of the following morning, nothing could shake our confidence, and already we were reaping a reward. The scenery as we climbed beyond the tree-line on the moraine was superb, and a touch of excitement was added by bear tracks. Wild goats had followed the same route up the glacier, keeping to the long trails of flint gravel on the lateral moraines. Ahead of us were mountains and passes in profusion – more than we wanted to see. Which, we wondered, would turn out to be the Muni La?

Towards noon we reached a point where the valley divided

into several branches and here our confidence received the first blow. Straight-ahead, where the map told us should have been the Muni La, lay a broad glacier saddle which clearly could not be used as a pass because the approach would involve climbing an extremely difficult ice-fall. Further to the right the saddles looked easier, but they would have taken us to the Darlang Nadi, a parallel valley further to the south leading back to Machail in one direction and towards the distant Poat La in the other. To the left, a cwm with a small glacier in it reared above inviting green slopes, and here we could imagine there might indeed be a pass though we could see no sign of a path leading towards it. And the cwm lay too far to the north, in the direction of the Umasi La.

What now? At first we were at a loss for an answer. Of course, it sometimes happens in the Alps that neither the map nor the existing literature enable a mountaineer to identify some feature that he is aiming for, an *arête*, say, or the approach to the foot of a rock wall, or the point where a traverse starts. On such occasions the rope team's discussion usually ends with a "Let's go and have a look!" And if that leads to nothing, at the worst only a couple of hours have been lost. But in our case, "Let's have a look" might have cost us days.

After careful thought, we chose the easier slopes on our left, leading up to the snow cwm. Here, if anywhere, we thought must be the route to the Muni La. The absence of visible tracks we explained by the fact that the pass had probably not been used for over a century.

After much labour – our rucksacks were definitely too heavy – we reached a point just before sunset about So yards below a fearsome-looking *arête*. So far there had been no technical obstacles, but now crevasses, ice-fall and *bergschrund* turned us plodding beasts of burden into battling mountaineers. At last we reached the sharp ridge, to sit there with the last rays of the sun on our backs, gazing at blue shadows creeping over a glacier deep in snow, flowing, as it seemed, in the wrong direction, towards the Darlang Nadi. There was no cairn or other sign of human presence on our col.

"We could bivouac over there," said Ludwig with moving unconcern, pointing to an island of scree on the far side of the glacier. This was the very thing we had sworn to avoid; hence we had left our air-beds behind. The late hour and the prospect of a cold night would not have mattered so much if we had found the pass, but obviously we were nowhere near it. The whole geography of the area seemed wrong. If this was the main ridge, as we thought, all the glaciers should have been flowing north-east, down to the Seni Nadi towards Zaskar; instead of which they were flowing south. Perhaps this was not the main ridge? There was little to cheer us as we settled ourselves for the night on a bed of hard, cold stones.

Early next morning we went up to the *névé* on a nearby saddle in the hope of seeing the lower course of our glacier. The snow was hard and the weather good, but the view was disappointing. We should have to climb higher still before we could decide on a route. However, there was one negative satisfaction: we could see now that the pass with the ice-fall would have led us to this same spot. We then climbed the first mountain in the same ridge. It took us forty-five minutes to reach the summit without rucksacks. From there we could see peak after peak and innumerable glaciers, but no sign of a pass crossing the main watershed. This was our second big surprise. The main Himalayan range obviously ran much further north than the old geographers had imagined. To eastward we could see several great secondary ridges stretching from north to south. If we had crossed them all in succession we must eventually have come to the main range and from there reached Zaskar; there were a good half-dozen passes inviting us. But we had come prepared to cross two passes, not six, and had brought barely enough fuel to cook a single meal of rice.

There was a small side-glacier starting from the snow *couloir* where we had left our rucksacks and flowing north with another saddle at its upper end leading, possibly, to the glaciers around the Umasi La. Here, we thought, was our only hope of reaching Zaskar. If that failed, the only alternative would be to descend over the huge glacier we had seen from the *arête* on the previous day turning right through an acute angle and leading back to the Darlang Nadi.

Though it was still early in the day the snow had already softened and half standing, half sitting, we managed to glissade down from the mountain in seven minutes. Having reached the bottom, we discovered that I had left my camera behind on the summit. Refraining from comment, we ate a little dried fruit and one or two leathery *chapátis* cooked by Ludwig three days before. Then, while he set out alone over the dangerously broken surface of the side-glacier for the "Pass of Good Hope", I started the climb to retrieve my camera.

By the time I caught up with Ludwig at the pass I felt thoroughly exhausted, not only by the climb itself but because the snow on the mountain slopes had meanwhile become miserably soft. While waiting, Ludwig had melted some ice for me and after rest and refreshment I climbed the last few yards to the ridge with him to examine what lay on the far side. Between us and the glacier there was a bare ice wall, perhaps 250 feet high. From time to time large lumps of snow were breaking away from the cornice on top of the ridge and hurtling down in an avalanche.

Ludwig pointed to the ice wall. "Do you think we could get down that? Over there must be the route from the Umasi La to Zaskar."

"No," I said somewhat peevishly. "I'm quite sure we couldn't, anyway, not with one and a half ice-axes and 20 yards of rope." Of course, we had no pitons, and no crampons either.

Laboriously we tapped our way back over the glacier to our starting point of that morning. Where Ludwig had walked across hard snow, and where ninety minutes later I had had to wade, there was now nothing but slush with crevices yawning up at us. By the time we reached our goal one whole valuable day, almost, had been wasted. The only alternative to returning ingloriously to Machail was now to explore the lower course of the glacier.

Though so far on this trip everything possible had gone wrong, the snags and disappointments provoked no kind of discord between Ludwig and myself. Yet he was fully entitled to an attitude of "I told you so!", for he had foreseen this trouble from the start. But there was no suggestion of that, not only because he exercised friendly restraint, but because our topographical problems had fired his enthusiasm. His sole thought now was to find out where all these north-south valleys did lead, and that only exploration could tell us. Meanwhile, he agreed to a very ambitious proposal, namely that we should try and climb down to the first birch trees before nightfall; his only qualification was a reminder that his legs were slightly shorter than mine.

And so we scrambled at top speed down the glacier, no doubt looking like a couple of frenzied travellers running to catch a train. Yet we managed to retain some indelible impressions: first, a large number of fan-shaped snow-fields with splendidly formed mountains at the interstices; then, a stream of ice flowing for miles between granite skyscrapers; and finally, a mass of granite blocks, each as big as a house, scattered in wild confusion over the tongue of the giant glacier lolling down like some precipitous mountain-slope. It might well have been that we were the first human beings ever to set eyes on this awe-inspiring scene. I shall never forget the crossing of that glacier. For hours on end we were stretched to the limit, wading through snow, jumping or getting round crevasses and streams of melting ice, picking our way across great medial moraines, finally scram-

Here and there we waded through fast-flowing ice-cold, glacial streams *(Fritz Kolb)*

bling, edging, clinging, leaping and balancing over and round the great blocks and boulders in the terminal moraine. In the last moments of daylight we saw a grey, level patch below us and made towards it. The twilight was brief and by the time we reached it, it was only by feeling with our hands that we could tell it was sand washed down and deposited there by the glacier stream. We pitched the tent at once. The ground was cold, but at least it was soft. It was too dark to find wood for a fire, so we had to do without a hot meal.

The following morning brought brilliant sunshine. In the distance we could see the flank of a mountain slanting away from us, indicating the main valley, probably the Darlang Nadi. There were no paths to be seen, but plenty of tracks, mostly of bears, foxes and hoofed animals. With each mile of the descent, the vegetation grew more luxuriant and soon we reached the first birch trees and signs of a nomad encampment. Towards noon we entered the main valley and close by a cave that had been used by shepherds made a huge fire of birch wood so that we could have a really big meal of rice. Before long the smoke attracted a visitor.

"What is the name of that valley?" asked Ludwig, speaking to the shepherd in Hindustani and pointing towards the main valley.

"Darlang Nadi, Sahib."

"How far is it from here to Machail?"

"One day, Sahib, if you start early in the morning."

So our fears had been justified!

"And what is the name of this side-valley, where your sheep are grazing?" asked Ludwig, pointing in the direction from which we had come.

"*Nam nahin hai, Sahib,*" came the reply. "It has no name."

*   *   *   *

What should we do now, we wondered. The Muni La did not exist. From the start we had ruled out the Poat La, at the head of the Darlang Valley, as being too far away. And this was the third day of the trip; we had already lost two days.

The most obvious course was to return to Machail, but I have never liked having to accept defeat when mountaineering, and by now Ludwig had become completely fired with the idea of the double Himalayan crossing. So, nevertheless, we talked in terms of the Poat La. We could save one day on the return by using the Umasi La. The villagers in Zaskar would be able to help us with food. But there was still the second lost day to make up for, and our original reason for rejecting the Poat La still held good – namely, that to cross into Zaskar by that pass would take us one day longer than we could afford – or, rather, than I could afford, for the time problem was mine, not Ludwig's. My wife was expected to arrive in Bombay on July 13. It was now June 28 and to reach Bombay in time I would have to start the journey from Machail on July 2 at the latest. So I now had three and a half days to spare, and no more.

Of course, it would have been possible to send my wife a telegram from somewhere on the journey to Bombay to tell her I would be late, but I could not bring myself to do that. If the Zaskar plan meant that I would not be on the landing-stage to meet her when she arrived, then, as far as I was concerned, Zaskar was out. When I told Ludwig this, he looked thoughtful and for some minutes after the shepherd had left us we sat on by the fire in silence. Then Ludwig began to talk. I cannot remember the arguments he used, but, looking at it now, I feel they must have been highly ingenious to have won me for the following plan:

Today, June 28, 1946. p.m.: walk about seventeen and a half miles to the foot of the Poat La.

June 29: cross the 18,800-foot pass and continue for sixteen and a quarter miles, as far as the valley of the Zaskar River.

June 30: cover thirty-two miles, including a 1,650-foot climb at the end of the day, to bivouac at the foot of the Umasi La.

July 1: cross the Umasi La (17,370 feet) and return to Machail, in all about twenty-five miles.

And then, for me: full speed, with porters, for the lowlands to catch the train to Bombay.

"... And you will just about get there in time," concluded Ludwig. Then he pledged his last ounce of energy to the fulfilment of this plan and in return I agreed to take the blame if we found there was no such pass as the Poat La or, alternatively, if we failed to find it.

Then we set off to cover the seventeen and a half miles to the foot of the Poat La. But though Ludwig's legs performed as promised and I, too, could have walked no faster, the Darlang

Nadi refused to come to an end. Soon it was clear that we could never reach the foot of the pass before dark and we shortened the day's goal to a distant bend in the valley from which we hoped it could be seen. But we lost so much time battling across a fierce mountain torrent that even the bend in the valley proved beyond our reach. Darkness was falling and we had to bivouac.

Was there a pass? We still did not know. There was a path going up the valley, but perhaps it only led to a grazing area. We had seen some sheep, but no shepherds. Where were they? And where were we? With these questions unanswered we climbed into our sleeping-bags, feeling lost in the vast wilderness of rock, ice and snow. Outside the tent towered the gigantic mountain walls separating the parallel valleys of the Darlang and the Chenab. Jagged smudges of glacier hung from the darkening sky. At that very site there was supposed to be a pass called the Kangla Jot. But if we had been aiming for it, we would have been no wiser than two days before, when we searched in vain for the Muni La. Both passes, perhaps, were no more than legends, or if they did exist, were miles away from the map references which the ancient geographers have given them from hearsay.

"It would be interesting," said Ludwig ironically, "to climb all these passes until we found which really did lead to the other side. We would then be able to put up a large notice board with KANGLA JOT on it." And would the same method show which pass was the Poat La? That was the unspoken question which troubled our dreams.

June 29. A misty day. For several hours we climbed as fast as we could up the path over the moraine, but still we were not round the corner. Himalayan glaciers need plenty of room in which to do their turns! When at last we reached the more level part of the glacier we found one of those terrors of the Himalayan mountaineer, a roaring cataract, barring our way. We had seen some yak droppings and so knew that the animals had come this way; presumably they had waded through the flood, ridden by their drovers. But what were we to do? I ventured in up to my waist, but if I had taken another step, the current would have swept me away.

So, once more, we faced an apparently impassable barrier. But this time, despite appearances, the gods were with us. Further down the moraine was a place where the surging torrent had struck and broken through some recently deposited debris, carrying all away except one huge boulder which remained perched high above the dirty, hissing waters. Over this precarious bridge we crossed – not without trepidation. Soon after, the path led down to the edge of the ice. A stone wall built as a shield against the weather, the ashes of a fire and animal droppings revealed the site where travellers regularly made their last bivouac before the pass. Full of hope, we steered out to the middle of the glacier, moving as briskly as we could. Owing to the time taken in crossing the cataract it was already long past noon.

It was raining and the top end of the glacier was hidden in cloud, but judging by its breadth, inclination and the state of the surface, the glacier would continue for several miles before we could hope to see *névé* or a pass. Tracks, of course, were not visible on the ice. Somehow, we had to *see* the pass, and for that we needed clear weather. Even then, there would have to be cairns or some sign of a track to indicate which of the many gullies and gaps in the ridge was the one leading to the promised land. We went hopping and panting over the ice, wasting few words.

Then, at this low ebb in our fortunes, came salvation. Two hundred yards ahead we saw men – seven Zaskaris with a dog.

"Where do you come from?" asked Ludwig.

"From Zaskar."

"Where is the pass?"

"Over there." A man in his forties, the only one who could speak Hindustani, pointed into the mist covering the right flank of the glacier bed.

"Is it far?"

"Yes, it is far," said the man. Then he added, little knowing the surprise he would cause: " – but from there to the second pass is not such a long way."

A second pass?

"This second pass," said Ludwig slowly, with a look at me, "can it be seen from the first?"

"But of course!"

It was now our turn to answer questions. Had we seen some nomad shepherds? The men wanted to buy wool. Would we give them away to the police in Zaskar? They had crossed the *jot*, the pass, illegally.

Ludwig reassured the men and we parted amicably, the Zaskaris continuing down towards the nearby bivouac while Ludwig and I started to climb a steep slope of ice and scree leading to the basin of a small subsidiary glacier. There were half a dozen of these side-valleys, one of them close beside us. We would never have guessed that a pass lay here, never have dreamt of exploring any of them. What luck!

But our loads were heavy, we were short of breath, the slope was steep and now the rain was turning to snow. Our enthusiasm began to evaporate. It was getting dark when we reached the horizontal snow-field at the top of the glacier and we could see no sign of the Zaskaris' tracks. Perhaps we had climbed the wrong glacier. Perhaps the man had meant the adjoining one – they both converged on the main glacier at the same point lower down. There was no hope of sighting the pass as the whole ridge was covered in cloud. Somehow we should have to find the tracks, and that meant searching systematically over the entire glacier.

Nearly exhausted, and very disgruntled, we split up, Ludwig exploring the left half of the glacier and I the right. The snow was like soft porridge and we were sinking in up to our knees. After a while Ludwig joined me on a small island of scree close to the edge of the glacier: he had found nothing and neither had I. By this time it was almost dark. We thought we would be more comfortable spending the night lower down, on the main glacier, so we turned our faces to the valley and braced ourselves for yet further effort.

We had just started the descent when Ludwig shouted: "Tracks!" And there, sure enough, in the scree, not in the snow, I could see footmarks. There was no doubt of it: this was the way the Zaskaris had come and naturally, as they were wearing moccasins, they had avoided the snow wherever possible and each man had carefully followed in the footsteps of the leader as he trod over the rubble.

But there are states of mind on which even a sudden stroke of good fortune fails to make an impression, and so it was with me. What mental struggles it had cost me on the previous day before I agreed to this Poat La adventure, this "plan" with its madcap

Then, at this low ebb in our fortunes, came salvation. Two hundred yards ahead we saw men — seven Zaskaris with a dog ... the only one who could speak Hindustani pointed into the mist *(Fritz Kolb)*

schedule! Of course it would never work. At this very moment, if I was to reach Bombay in time, I should have been on the other side of the Himalayas, in bivouac. Instead of which, we were at the north end of some pass which we could not see and would probably have to spend hours searching for on the morrow before we could even cross it. And then we calmly intended to start looking for a second pass!

But Ludwig was in a different mood. The discovery of the tracks had rekindled his enthusiasm for the whole trip and no doubt in his mind's eye he was once more seeing Zaskar, a piece of Tibet, and, leading to it, the pass over the greatest mountain barrier in the world that no white man had ever trodden before. With such a prize dangling before him, what did a couple of days matter, more or less?

"Fritz," said Ludwig cautiously, "do you think it will be so very much warmer if we bivouac down there on the main glacier?" In other words: Don't you think we had better go on to Zaskar, now that we have found these tracks and know that the pass exists?

A minute later, our bulging rucksacks were on the ground and we were collecting large flat stones covered with tough verglas to build a platform for the tent. The tent was soon up and even at this height of over 16,500 feet it proved its worth. But it was a cheerless night: wet socks, damp boots, no proper food, little fuel and, outside, darkness and bad weather.

In every mountaineering team there is always someone who has to break the rules. On this trip it was Ludwig. Before leaving Machail we had agreed to leave behind the ground-sheet which we usually spread on the floor of the tent. Now, without a word, he drew it from his rucksack and laid it over the scree. A gross breach of discipline, particularly as I had been carrying the heavier rucksack all the way! But I could not summon up the hypocrisy to pretend I was not pleased. And even with the ground-sheet, the night was bad enough. I started by lying on my back, and when that began to freeze, I turned over on to my left side. Soon the spectre of rheumatism in left knee, hip and shoulder drove me on to my stomach, until various internal organs began to protest, then – over on to the right side. Five minutes later I was on my back again. That accounted for half an hour. But the whole night lasted for ten.

June 30. If you spend a sleepless night at home you are reluctant to get out of bed in the morning. But we were up at the first light of dawn with the alacrity of men escaping the torture chamber. What trials could the day hold compared with those we had just survived? All the same, it proved arduous.

When we looked out of the tent we could see nothing but clouds and slanting snow-flakes. Above us, the wind was moaning over the ridge. From the top end of the scree we slowly and laboriously followed the Zaskaris' tracks in the snow. They were only just visible. They seemed to lead up to our right, to where, high over our heads, a strong wind was blowing the snow from some strange-looking towers which turned out to be cleverly built cairns. The steep slope separating us from them tested us to the limit of our strength. As long as we were on snow the going was tolerable, but when we had to climb up loose scree and flat, smooth slate with no holds, we had to regain our balance after each step and the unwieldy loads on our backs made this almost impossible. At an altitude of 18,700 feet, we – and I, in particular – found this scramble-lurch-and-totter no joke.

On leaving the bivouac we had still possessed one slab of chocolate, but I had lost my half to Ludwig in a bet about the Zaskaris' tracks. Now, as we stood at last on the wind-swept pass, he must have realized that I was all-in, for, as an act of kindness which sounds obvious in retrospect but meant a lot at the time, he insisted on me eating it. But in those days we still possessed the inexhaustible reserves that belong to the first half of life, and a few moments' rest, and a couple of nuts and currants from the rucksack were enough to restore my strength.

As the Zaskaris had said, we could now see the second pass, or at least glimpse it through gaps in the clouds. The ridge was not accessible at the same spot from the Tibetan side as from the Indian. Between us and the place where the Zaskans had come up from the north-east lay a difficult section of the ridge, about 175 yards long with rock towers and steep ice-walls. How the Zaskaris had managed to scale it without ice-axes or climbing boots was a mystery. We found it easier to force a direct descent to the glacier, with step-kicking and safeguards against slipping on the wet snow. After that, there were some dangerous crevices to be circumvented and then we found ourselves wading out through increasingly watery snow on to the broad, white surface of a piedmont glacier. Around us stood strangely shaped mountains announcing the new world of Inner Asia. As we progressed the weather steadily improved. The huge glacier which served as our path and guide was now showing every sign of disintegration: giant glacier tables, whole rows of moulins and an extremely rough surface. Shortly after midday the whole of it, including the dangerous convex tongue, was behind us. Then, once more, by some massive cubes of rock, we saw burnt out fires and yak droppings. This was the camp site on the north-east side of the Poat La, a place marked "Kanjur" on the map. As we rested, a watery sun came out to greet us.

Could yaks be taken over the pass? It seemed unlikely, though they were certainly used on both sides, up to the last camp sites.

Throughout that afternoon we kept going without a stop until we were almost out into the main valley. Beyond noticing that it was entirely different, we had little time to look at the scenery as we were straining every nerve to reach the objective which should have been attained twenty-four hours before. This time it was Ludwig who came near to exhaustion. When we finally halted I asked him to leave the evening's work to me so that he could recover his strength for the no less strenuous marches to come.

In such circumstances, at the end of a tiring day, mountaineers have to resist the temptation to lie down and go to sleep just anywhere and anyhow. It is important to make the bivouac as comfortable as possible, to eat and drink one's fill on the best fare available, and to cool and refresh the skin, particularly the feet. Our first bivouac beyond the Himalayas fulfilled all these requirements in that the hay of a fern-like creeping plant supplied plenty of soft, warm bedding and *burza* was available in unlimited quantities. *Burza* is the name given to the ligneous tubers of the diminutive juniper tree and is the only substance to be found in the valleys of Tibet that can be used as fuel. Birch trees grow only on the southern slopes of the Himalayas.

Between gulps of heavily sweetened tea we demolished an imposing mass of spiced rice and vegetables. Then we sat back and took a long look at the clear, vivid colours of the Tibetan landscape and let the hush of evening, backed by the distant rustle of glacier streams, sink into our ears. Here, low down in the valley, the shadows had long since gathered, but far away, beneath a cloudless sky, the mountain ridges glowed violet in the sunset. Despite our fatigue our minds were awake and receptive, and gradually we began to sense that, like some simple opening theme in a symphony, this perfect evening was the prelude to a day we should long remember.

July 1, 1946. After a restful night we awoke refreshed, but feeling lazy and reluctant to leave our luxury beds. Our shoulders still ached from the rucksack, and our legs were as heavy as lead.

We had not been walking long when we were halted by an impressive scene. Rearing up from the shadows still lying in the valley of the Zarap-Lingti-Chu was a great cliff with a domed summit crowned by a Buddhist monastery. The bottom of the valley and most of a vast mountain flank on the far side were still

Rearing up from the shadows still lying in the valley of the Zarap-Lingti-Chu was a great cliff with a domed summit crowned by a Buddhist monastery, but as we watched the sun topped a distant ridge and a single shaft struck down, spotlighting the fortress walls, the battlements aflutter with white and yellow prayer-flags *(Fritz Kolb)*

in shadow but, as we watched, the sun topped a distant ridge and, a single shaft struck down, spot-lighting the fortress walls, the battlements, aflutter with white and yellow prayer-flags, and the buildings huddled below. Gradually the sunlight spread until the whole cliff and the scrub-covered slopes of the mountain behind were flooded with brilliance.

We now entered the main valley, following a broad pathway which led along one side. At home it would have been called a cart-track, but in this part of the world the wheel has not yet been invented and carts are unknown. The people ride or go on foot, carrying their loads themselves or tying them on the backs of their animals. In the course of thousands of years the stones on the pathway had been worn round and smooth. Between them lay hot, white shimmering sand. Briar-roses in massive flower stood by the wayside. Soon a fiery sun was scorching our backs while the bare mountains ahead reflected the light into our faces. There was not a tree, not a shadow, anywhere. Though the area lies 12,000 feet above sea-level, that in itself would not prevent the growth of vegetation. The enemy is dryness. The Himalayas catch the rain clouds and their slopes and folds channel the rainwater into the Indian rivers which irrigate the crops for four hundred million people. For the valleys of Inner Asia not a drop is left. They are waterless, arid. Fields of barley and a few stunted trees which we saw at the mouth of a tributary valley owed their existence to a trickle diverted from a mountain stream, while the stream itself drew its water from the slowly melting glaciers.

The people use yak-dung as a fuel and follow the glacier streams for miles to collect dry brushwood. Their houses are built of stone or mud. But beams are needed for the flat roofs and they, presumably, are fetched from far distant places.

Towards midday we reached Padum, the capital of Zaskar. When we entered the village it seemed deserted, but suddenly we found ourselves surrounded by a crowd that must have comprised the entire population. Some of the people spoke Hindustani, which is the *lingua franca* between the Brahmaputra, the Indus and the Godawari.

"Where have you come from?" they asked.

"*Jot se* – from the pass," we said, pointing towards the Poat La.

"Where are you heading for?"

When we entered the village it seemed deserted, but suddenly we found ourselves surrounded by a crowd that must have comprised the entire population *(Fritz Kolb)*

"For Machail, over the other pass. Have you got porters for us?"

"*Ho sakta* – it is possible. When do you wish to start?"

"We wish to start now, at this very moment."

"When do you wish to be in Machail?"

"Tomorrow," said Ludwig.

Tomorrow! The man who had spoken turned to his companions and we saw them murmuring and shaking their heads together. Then he addressed us in Hindustani again

"In that case, you will die. No one here will go with you. No one here wishes to die with you."

And now we could get no porters even to go with us to the next village. The good people of Padum must have thought we were mad to be in such a hurry – they knew nothing about trains, and still less about ships arriving in Bombay. And the fact that we Sahibs had no servants with us must already have struck them as odd. But they soothed us with buttermilk and wonderful barley bread, and refused any payment. They also said "No" to our enquiry for more. We asked whether there was a shop in the village. Not in this village, they said, but there was one in Suru, five days' journey away to the west.

Each village in this area has to be self-supporting between harvests. Despite our wolf's hunger, Ludwig and I could never have eaten the Padumers out of hearth and home, but that can easily happen when big expeditions with hundreds of porters arrive. Often, on such occasions, the dwellers in many a Himalayan valley have been unable to resist the proffered silver and have sold all their food with the result that winter has brought with it starvation, robbery and murder. So in due course the British restricted the number of expeditions visiting each area to one a year.

The ice-axe, our felt hats, and especially Ludwig's boots with their Tricouni nails were closely examined and much admired, the Padumers besieging him with questions which he seemed to enjoy answering. Ludwig's Hindustani vocabulary was considerable. Meanwhile, I took photographs. A camera was obviously no novelty to these people, for as soon as they saw mine, they started posing, one of them even climbing on to a boulder and holding up his arms to attract attention.

The afternoon was more suffering than joy. Though a Zaskari horseman carried our rucksacks for part of the way, we felt inordinately tired. For walking in the valleys I had brought with me a pair of ordinary boots with rubber soles. Having found on previous trips how tiring it could be to slide about on smooth stones in nailed boots, I had thought it worth carrying the extra weight. But Ludwig did not share this opinion and so only had his climbing boots with him. He had no easy time of it that afternoon.

The vast floor of the valley seemed to stretch into infinity. We plodded on and on, but apparently made no progress. The landmarks barely moved. Here and there we had to wade through fast flowing streams. Then a little black dot appeared in the distance and slowly came towards us – a traveller on horseback. At last, we met. Dismounting, he walked past us, made a silent and dignified salutation, then climbed on his horse and half an hour later had dwindled to the same black dot.

Now and again we came to farm buildings and grazing yaks. An old man twirling his prayer-wheel was quite willing to be

"Then a little black dot appeared in the distance and slowly came towards us
– a traveller on horseback. At last we met. Dismounting, he walked past us,
made a silent and dignified salutation, then climbed on his horse and half an hour later
had dwindled to the same black dot" *(Fritz Kolb)*

photographed. Thousands of stones lay carefully piled by the wayside, inscribed with the sacred words: *Om mani padme hum* – "Oh! The jewel in the lotus!"

And the sun rode slowly across the sky, passed us and sank towards the mountain ridges on the western horizon. At last we were in Ating at the north foot of the Umasi La. The horseman gave us our rucksacks. We stopped for a while to eat, then started to climb up towards the pass.

* * * *

How tired we were! The bridle path climbed steeply up the valley over bare, uninteresting slopes. Behind us, a snow-free mountain glowed with unearthly splendour in the last rays of the setting sun. Higher up, we had to cross a torrent that came foaming down in a number of separate streams over a slope of coarse scree. Soon after, rock walls forced us right down to the main river, now swollen by the ice that had melted during the day, and then into the water itself where we went hopping over stones spaced at intervals and now lying well below the surface of the river. Later on, the valley broadened again and there was room to pitch the tent where we chose. The day's goal was really a camp site called Gaura, but it would have taken a good hour to reach it and we could not resist the temptation to bivouac where we were.

When it came to getting a meal, I found that the cooking-pot was missing from my rucksack and, with it, a small bag that I kept inside containing our travel documents and all our money. It was a terrible shock. The pot was usually stowed under the flap, right on top of my rucksack. Where was it now … ? When something has been lost, people usually ask: When did you last see it? And, as usual when the thing is a familiar article that one normally takes for granted, I was unable to remember. But I presumed I had forgotten to buckle the pot under the flap again after removing it from its place when getting some food out of the sack, or fixing the boots on to it before wading a stream. But where? In Ating, at the foot of the pass? Or earlier, as far back as Padum … ?

The loss of the money was so serious that I felt it was a waste of time racking my memory when, in any case, I could not be sure where it had occurred. So, full of desperate resolve, I took the ice-axe and a lantern and in the last glimmer of daylight started back for Ating. The first place where I could hope to find anything, was by the ford at the last stream we had crossed. That was about an hour's walk away, further down the valley, but to reach it I would first have to cross the submerged stepping-stones in the main river, and in pitch darkness that would obviously be impossible. Even on dry land I was stumbling more than enough. So, realising I was on a fool's errand, I turned back.

For the rest of that evening Ludwig and I concentrated on

An old man twirling his prayer-wheel was quite willing to be photographed *(Fritz Kolb)*

three objects: we tried to avoid worrying our heads over where the loss had occurred, avoid thinking of the shepherds who had been grazing their sheep near the ford in the stream, and avoid spending a bad night through fear of not waking early enough next morning. Thanks to long practice in self-discipline, all this was achieved. But neither of us dared broach the subject of the next day's schedule. It involved crossing the Umasi La and marching from there to Machail.

July 2, 1946. I awoke quite naturally at 3 a.m. and left Ludwig five minutes later with the urgent request that he should sleep for another hour. An hour later, I was gazing, weak with relief, at the cooking-pot and, vastly more important, at its contents where it lay, abandoned and untouched, amidst a mass of stones at the precise spot where we had taken off our boots before wading the stream.

When I got back to Ludwig with my big "Yes!", I found he had done all the morning chores. The tent was packed up. The two fat rucksacks, those instruments of torture, were standing side by side, mocking us, and in our second-best cooking-pot was a dubious concoction which I hastily swallowed. It was late – we had no time to lose.

The day was dull, but the visibility was good. This time, we were certain that the pass we were heading for really did exist. A clearly marked track went snaking up between the rocks on the valley floor and some straw sandals lying abandoned beside it showed that it was frequented by human beings. In Machail they had told us that everyone in the Padar region took five pairs of these sandals with him when he went over the pass. Beside a babbling stream, lush cushions of grass were growing, dotted with clumps of edelweiss and Alpine asters in full flower.

The glacier coming down the north side of the pass was short and harmless. As we approached it, a flock of sheep were leaping and sliding down a steep snow-field. To our left we saw the ice ridge on which we had stood six days before without being able to descend.

It was not until after the midday rest that we came to the place where the beaten track led out on to the glacier. Laboriously but in confident mood, we took it in turns to kick steps in the snow, which became steeper the nearer we got to the saddle. At 5 p.m. we set foot for the second time on the main watershed. As though to mark the occasion, the sun broke through the clouds. We sat down to rest by a number of sacred Buddhist objects in stone and iron which lay in heaps, decorating the mountain gateway to India.

The Umasi La is 17,370 feet high. Yet at intervals throughout the summer, sheep are herded across the pass from south to north, where their wool is traded for salt. Compared with this annual exchange which has taken place since time immemorial between the peoples of Padar and the Zaskaris, who are their nearest neighbours on the other side of the mountains, only a fraction of the traffic across the Umasi La consists of travellers from distant countries. The pass is one of the main links between Leh in the Upper Indus Valley and the valley of the Chenab. Travellers from Leh to Jammu must use it. Yet the name Umasi La is unknown both in Ating on the north side and in Machail on the south. Similarly, no one in Padum had heard of the Poat La. To them, both passes were simply the *jot* – that is, the "pass". I do not know the origin of the names Umasi La and Poat La, which are those given on the map. Were they perhaps introduced by the ancient Chinese geographers who centuries ago reached India by the land route?

* * * *

The glaciers on the south side of the Himalayas are longer and larger than those on the northern slopes. This axiom Ludwig and I can vouch for from bitter experience. It was late and we kept moving as fast as we could. To start with, we sank up to our knees in the softened snow. The sheep tracks were of no use to us. Later, we were confronted with steeper slopes where there were more crevices and where we sank even deeper into the snow. On reaching the snow-line we got our first view of the whole glacier. It was a superb sight. Under low, heavy clouds (presaging the monsoon), the stream of ice flowed broad and majestically towards the south-west. Its length caused us mixed feelings. Night was coming on and we were both severely fatigued.

After some miles of jumping over crevices, glacier streams and *séracs*, Ludwig sat down, desperately cursing himself for having cramp in the leg. But, as I assured him, no excuses were needed. Had not I felt just as bad, at the Poat La, for instance, while he had still been comparatively fresh? And years before, on a Swiss glacier, I had heard a famous sprinter groaning with cramp just as loudly as he. But friendly words did not bring me to the end of my resources – far from it. In the midst of the glacier ice, regardless of threatening clouds and gathering darkness, the rebellious muscles were suitably patted, kneaded and stroked, from the heel to the buttock, as I had learnt as an athlete – and with favourable results.

With Ludwig once more in the running, we climbed over a mountainous pile of horribly loose rubble in a moraine and by nightfall reached a point where the track from the pass branched off from the glacier. I then put on my rubber-soled boots and went scurrying down as fast as I could in the hope of reaching the floor of the valley and a good site for the bivouac before the last gleam of daylight had vanished. Ludwig followed slowly. But as each rock wall dropped behind me, another and deeper one appeared below, and still no point was visible in the black abyss where the descent would come to an end. Better a bad bivouac together, I thought, than the agony of losing each other in the dark, and so I waited for Ludwig to catch up. Then slowly we went on together, feeling our way down. The thin sickle of a day-old moon stood clear and beautiful in the sky. In an hour it would be gone.

And now we could hear the roaring of that same river where we had stood a week before, searching in vain for a crossing. There, in the darkness below, lay familiar territory, with level campsites, birch tees, fuel. If only we could reach it ....

It was pitch dark and there were about fifty yards to go when we lost the path. The slopes were still steep, but the river was now just discernible as a faint gleam where its waters went foaming over the rocks. We edged down a little further, going slow, very slowly, very conscious of that adage about the cup and the lip. Then we switched on the tiny electric torch, so carefully saved up, and searched – and found the path, and went down the last few yards to reach safety on the valley floor. It was midnight.

We had not the strength to make comfortable beds or even pitch the tent. We simply laid it out and covered ourselves with a fold. But first, we made a meal, of a kind, from scraps and ate a little, then threw the rest away. It rained during the night and we slept badly.

July 3, 1946. In dull, misty monsoon weather we wandered slowly down to Machail, taking nearly the whole day for a walk that we had previously done in hours. Admittedly, we spent some time at the first farm we came to in Bujwas, eating and drinking our fill of sour milk and *chapátis*, and that episode has remained in my memory as the bright spot, the only one, in the concluding day of our trip.

*   *   *   *

Between our arrival in Machail and the end of our foot journey at the bus terminus in Bhadarwar lay another seven days' hike – days of strenuous walking as we were in a great hurry, but easy, nevertheless, compared with the trip we had just finished.

I say "we", but it was I who was short of time; Ludwig merely suited his plans to mine. He would have liked to cross the Pir Panjal chain from Atholi, as Fabian had done, rightly thinking that from there we would be able to look back over the area we had visited and see more of its geography. According to the map, it would have taken us no longer to reach Bhadarwar by that route than by going through Kishtwar. On the other hand, we should have to take a whole day's rest before attempting another pass; the ridge of the Pir Panjal chain was now covered in monsoon cloud; and I remembered that Fabian had found diffi-culty in obtaining porters. For these reasons I could not bring myself to yield to Ludwig's entreaties.

As far as Kishtwar, therefore, we followed the same route as before. From the great bridge at Atholi I solemnly dropped my climbing boots – worn out by now and totally useless – into the milky waters of the Chenab, thinking as I did so of the king in Goethe's poem, *Der König in Thule*. Meanwhile, we were slowly recovering from our exhaustion. The first eggs worked wonders and I became convinced that we had failed to provide for enough albumen in our diet and that my lapses of memory, unusual for me, over the cooking-pot and the camera were a result of albumen deficiency.

The feeling that our walk through the Chenab Valley up to Bhadarwar would probably be the last I should ever see of the Himalayas counteracted the effects of physical tiredness and heightened my perceptions. I rejoiced in the diversity of the butterflies, trees and flowers, gazed once more on the grandeur of the hanging valleys – the product of slow erosion of the main valleys by glaciers – and enjoyed again the company of the simple, unspoilt people who went with us as porters. All nine of them were wearing greyish-white garments of coarse goat's hair, bright red cummerbunds and the helmet-shaped headgear universally worn in this part of the Himalayas, made of white woollen material with a thin edging of red.

They were excellent fellows. If they had not all been away, herding their sheep over the Umasi La, when we arrived at Machail on May 31, they might have helped us after all to climb The Sickle Moon mountain. Wherever they went, they carried their loads without a word of complaint, willingly walked the long distances we set as our daily goal and were always ready to regale our rests with song. When we pitched our tent in the evenings, they cheerfully lay down on the bare ground, wherever it was, put their loads between their legs, drew up a blanket and slept peacefully until morning.

"Why do you put your packs between your legs?" we asked.

"In case of thieves, Sahib," they politely replied.

Our porters had declined from the start to go further than Kishtwar, so from there to Bhadarwar we had to hire two horses. It took us a valuable half-day to arrange for the animals and then only one turned out to be a horse. The other was a miserably thin donkey. After two or three hours the donkey broke down and the horse had to carry its load. We were terrified that the horse would then collapse, but it survived the two days' march, though early on the second day, Ludwig had to run on ahead to hold the bus in case I should fail to coax drover, horse and lingering donkey to the bus-stop on time.

So ended the third Himalayan journey. We were only one day behind schedule and that I could make up by juggling with train connections. Ludwig discovered, incidentally, that he should already have been in the schoolroom correcting exercises, and also that he could not pay his fare back to Udaipur. But such trivialities disturb only Westerners with their exaggerated sensibilities; with goodwill on all sides we found they could be easily settled.

I said goodbye to Ludwig in Lahore, goodbye until — ? We little knew then how far our ways would diverge. Today he is in New Zealand. We have both become fathers of families.

When I reached Bombay, Fabian told me that the troopship bringing my wife to India had been a week late in sailing. So, after all, I had come too early. The days of waiting dragged on.

The monsoon had started and the air was saturated with moisture. Sunshine alternated with rain. When at last the moment arrived. I armed myself with an umbrella and went out on to the quay. Slowly the tall ship edged in towards the wall. On deck, clusters of passengers were standing, craning their necks to recognize the friends who had come to meet them. Soon, hands and handkerchiefs were fluttering, among them that same hand that I had last seen, waving farewell to me on Vienna station, seven years before.

Bibliography

Some of the scientific and technical aspects of the author's experiences in the Himalayas are treated in greater detail in the following:

English works

The Himalayan Journal, Vol. XIII, 1946. (L. Krenek, "The Mountains of Central Lahul.")

The Himalayan Journal, Vol. XIV, 1947. (F. Kolb, "Third Choice – Adventures in the Padar Region.")

The Indian Geographical Journal, Vol. XX, 1945. (L. Krenek, "Recent and Past Glaciation of Lahul.")

The Punjab Geographical Review, Vol. III, 1948. (L. Krenek, "Some Exploration East and West of the Umasi La.")

German works

Fels und Firn, 1949, Series 1 and 2, and also 1950, Series I (Vienna): L. Krenek, Erschliessungsfahrten im Pandschab-Himalaya.

Indien heute, by L. Krenek, Volksbuchverlag, Vienna. (1953).

Also from Sigma Leisure:

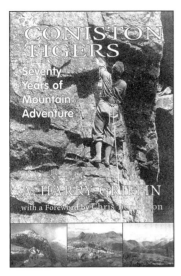

THE CONISTON TIGERS – Seventy Years of Mountain Adventure
A. Harry Griffin

This is the life story of A Harry Griffin MBE, much loved as Country Diary writer for The Guardian. As much of interest to lovers of the great outdoors, and to those who simply enjoy writing of the highest calibre, "The Coniston Tigers" features period photographs of climbers from the 1930s with their minimal climbing gear – some nonchalantly smoking their pipes as they balance on the most delicate ledge.
"A very special book . . .a living history of Modern Lakeland climbing" – Chris Bonington. "The book which thousands have been willing Harry Griffin to write." – Alan Rusbridger, Editor of The Guardian. "Prose tumbles off the page as clear as a mountain stream – a classic of mountain literature" – Bill Birkett, mountain writer & photographer. "Harry Griffin is one of the great outdoor writers of the century." – Cameron McNeish, Editor of The Great Outdoors. *£9.95*

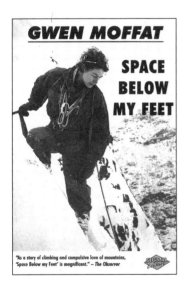

SPACE BELOW MY FEET
Gwen Moffat

"As a story of climbing and compulsive love of mountains, Space Below my Feet is magnificent." – The Observer.

This is a republication of a classic book about mountains, men and love. It tells how Gwen Moffat, an army deserter, made her uninhibited, unconventional way to become Britain's leading female climber, and the first woman to qualify as a mountain guide. There are acutely observed accounts of mountaineering exploits, as she tackles the toughest climbs.

A book full of warm, human stories to demonstrate the bonds between climbers and the relationships that developed. Illustrated with striking mountain landscape photographs to demonstrate Gwen Moffat's remarkable climbing ability. Of great interest to all who love the great outdoors, and to everybody who finds real-life stories far more fascinating than fiction. *£8.95*

All of our books are available through booksellers. In case of difficulty, or for a free catalogue, please contact: SIGMA LEISURE, 1 SOUTH OAK LANE, WILMSLOW, CHESHIRE SK9 6AR.
Phone: 01625-531035; Fax: 01625-536800; E-mail: info@sigmapress.co.uk
Web site: http//www.sigmapress.co.uk
MASTERCARD and VISA orders welcome.